Rosslyn Revealed

ROSSLYN REVEALED

Alan Butler and John Ritchie

BOOKS

Winchester, U.K.
New York, U.S.A.

First published by O Books, 2006
O Books is an imprint of John Hunt Publishing Ltd.,
The Bothy, Deershot Lodge, Park Lane, Ropley, Hants, SO24 0BE, UK
office1@o-books.net
www.o-books.net

Distribution in:

UK and Europe
Orca Book Services
orders@orcabookservices.co.uk
Tel: 01202 665432
Fax: 01202 666219 Int. code (44)

USA and Canada
NBN
custserv@nbnbooks.com
Tel: 1 800 462 6420
Fax: 1 800 338 4550

Australia and New Zealand
Brumby Books
sales@brumbybooks.com.au
Tel: 61 3 9761 5535
Fax: 61 3 9761 7095

Far East (offices in Singapore,
Thailand, Hong Kong, Taiwan)
Pansing Distribution Pte Ltd
kemal@pansing.com
Tel: 65 6319 9939
Fax: 65 6462 5761

South Africa
Alternative Books
altbook@peterhyde.co.za
Tel: 021 447 5300
Fax: 021 447 1430

Text copyright Alan Butler and John Ritchie 2006

Design: Jim Weaver

ISBN-13: 978 1 905047 92 5
ISBN-10: 1 905047 92 4

A CIP catalogue record for this book is available from the British Library.

Printed in the US by Maple Vail

Dedication

To the memory of the late Michael Bentine
who, long before almost anyone else, was
wise enough to suggest that the real treasure
of Rosslyn Chapel lay in its carvings.

Acknowledgements

It is never easy to write a list of acknowledgments, many people have helped us, and if we leave anyone out then we offer our sincere apologies.

We would like to offer our sincere thanks to:

Our families: Kate Butler – who was always on hand and who was a wizard with the indexing. Catriona and Hynde Ritchie for their patience, and encouragement.

To the magnanimous magister and our good friend Henry Lincoln; the evergreen and ever generous Niven Sinclair and Judy Fisken who was always kind enough to give her time and knowledge. We would also like to thank the incredible Pat Napier who always seemed to find written source material that no one was aware of, Scott Grant for his web skills and technical wisdom and George Hynd for listening with a Masonic ear.

Thanks also to Stuart and Simon Beattie, Nancy Bruce, and all the excellent guides and staff at Rosslyn Chapel for their patience, enthusiasm and generosity.

We also need to acknowledge Dr Barbara Crawford of St Andrews University whose work on the early Orkney Sinclairs is second to none and Dr Jonathan A. Glenn for his scholarly work on Sir Gilbert Haye.

A special thanks to our publisher John Hunt – for service above and beyond the call of duty and to our Literary Agent Fiona Spencer-Thomas, who not only helps us all the way but who also knows some great restaurants in London.

Our gratitude also goes to Filip Coppens, who was generous with his knowledge.

Chris Knight – for his great assistance with our research, Robert Bryden for his encouragement and esoteric wisdom, Joy and John Millar of the Sauniere Society for their encouragement, Mrs Clark for the use of her family archive. Douglas Ritchie, Charlie Napier, George Campbell, Joy Madden, George Peaston, and the people of the village of Roslin.

We also freely acknowledge our debt to the Earls of Rosslyn for having the foresight to preserve and restore such a historical treasure, and finally Earl William Sinclair and Sir Gilbert Haye who left us such a rich archive of knowledge from which to work.

Rosslyn Revealed DVD

For those readers who wish to explore our findings in picture form we have created a DVD, which also includes spoken dialogue by both Alan Butler and John Ritchie. For further details and how to order see our website at **www.rosslynrevealed.com**

Contents

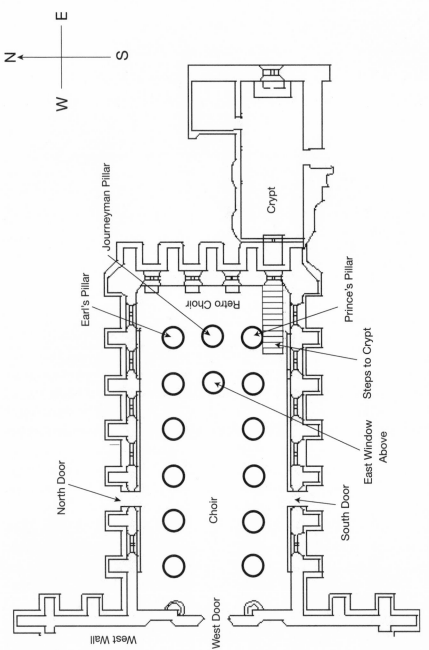

Floor plan of Rosslyn Chapel showing the various parts of the building

Introduction

THIS BOOK IS the result of many years of combined research, from very different directions. John was born in Roslin and, despite a busy life as a film cameraman and programme maker, has been constantly drawn back to the chapel, gradually making himself into one of the foremost experts on the building. He has collected thousands of photographs, read everything he could about the place and conducted exhaustive historical research, both into the chapel itself and the period during which it was created.

Alan has been a professional author for more than twenty years. With a penchant for astronomy and history, Alan has published books on the ancient civilization of the Minoans and co-written a book on the evolution of European measuring systems. Working with Canadian writer Stephen Dafoe he has also conducted extensive research into the Knights Templar, a co-operation that resulted in two books. There have been further books about the evolution of modern religions. Included amongst these are *The Goddess, the Grail and the Lodge* and *The Virgin and the Pentacle*.

We were each drawn to Rosslyn Chapel for different reasons; John, because the Chapel has always been a part of his life. Running, as he does, the Edinburgh Guide website, and contributing to innumerable film and television programmes, he also has a natural interest in key sites around Edinburgh. Alan, meanwhile, has always been fascinated by the byways and undercurrents of history, and nowhere do these seem to rise so close to the surface as in the Rosslyn Chapel.

There have been endless speculations, often seemingly fantastic, about what this extraordinary building represents, and what hidden treasures might lie there. Since the publication of *The Da Vinci Code* in 2005, which features the Chapel in the climax of the book and the film, the worldwide interest in the building has been enormous. But as the recent court case over questions of plagiarism indicated, the author Dan Brown was drawing on ideas that had been in currency for some time.

When we started to pool our research twelve years ago we tried to keep open minds, prepared to come to the conclusion that the building was nothing more than sceptics and mainstream historians generally claim; in other words that it is simply the truncated remnants of what was originally planned as a larger but quite ordinary church, albeit one with highly elaborate decoration. However, since our co-operation began, drawing on original documents and allowing the Chapel to speak to us, we have made many original discoveries. Some of our extraordinary findings relate to the people who built the Chapel, others to its construction. This latter culminated earlier this year in our discovery of a "light box" above the East Window of the chapel, a unique and important finding that we outline in this book for the first time.

There are many starting points for writing on the Rosslyn Chapel, but let us be clear from the outset. The more we learnt about it, and the greater our exploration of the undercurrents of religious and philosophical thought in the 15th century, the more we came to see the chapel as something far from a normal church. In so far as the Chapel is a place of worship, we came to see it as representing a far more diverse, open, intellectually tolerant and curious strand of Christianity than the one that became predominant in the West. Rosslyn Chapel represents a genuinely alternative tradition, one closer to Christianity's Judaic roots – a belief that is more philosophical, more embracing in its approach to other traditions, and indeed one that has just as good a claim as the presently accepted version of Christianity to represent the thinking and beliefs of the first Christians.

This may upset some visitors and readers. But the intellectual landscape regarding the origins of Christianity has changed radically over the last few decades, particularly since the discovery of the Dead Sea Scrolls. Virtually no serious scholar now claims that the Christianity we know today came down to us unadulterated from Jesus and his disciples. It was the result of one version of history and belief triumphing over others. The opinion of the vast majority of scholars is that what we now know as Christianity was established over a period of many centuries, taking particular expression (in its Western form at least) in the various Church Councils from the 4th to 9th centuries AD. All experts would accept that in the first couple of centuries there were a number of very diverse traditions competing for acceptance, and the choice of which gospels and doctrines would be mainstream and which heresy was a question of ecclesiastical and state politics, at a time when it was impossible to separate the two. We can now see with startling clarity that the 'sort' of Christianity we have come to accept was more a question of "power" than "truth". Though Christian scholars prefer to interpret these processes as the Holy Spirit working through the councils of men.

All of this is now beyond serious dispute. What we do suggest here, and though the argument is genuinely controversial it is supported by our original research, is that one of the many, early, alternative forms of Christianity survived the persecution of its orthodox brethren. It did so not just in the Near and Middle East but also in Western Europe, where it found its most complete and lasting expression in Rosslyn Chapel. Without understanding these ideas that fed into its construction, Rosslyn Chapel will remain a mystery.

Admittedly, there are no existing historical documents along the lines of "I built this chapel because I believe this". But then there are no original documents of the Old or New Testament either. What we have is carefully collected evidence, drawing on as many reliable historical sources as possible. Ultimately this is what all history represents. We hope to persuade you that our version of events is the most plausible.

It is unlikely that we would ever be able to demonstrate, without any grain of doubt, what really motivated the builders of this fantastic structure. Rosslyn Chapel was built at a time when anything deviating from orthodoxy was viewed with suspicion and when such deviant notions as those expressed within its walls could have resulted in its architects being tortured and burned at the stake. But it was also built in a period when there was a small but significant window of opportunity. Its construction became possible through the meeting of a few extraordinary individuals, the vicissitudes of European politics at the time the building was commenced, and, underlying everything, the gradual erosion of the authority of a fierce feudal Church that had held all of Christendom in its grip for centuries.

With no insult intended to Dan Brown, author of *The Da Vinci Code*, we dare to suggest that truth really is stranger than fiction. Our conclusions may seem astonishing, but they are backed by so many solid, first-hand discoveries that we have no hesitation in setting them out in this Introduction, ahead of the presentation of our evidence.

Our story covers the background of the most powerful and wealthy individual in the Scotland of his day, William Sinclair. It was he who provided the finance for the Chapel. We also look closely at one of Scotland's most learned sons, Sir Gilbert Haye, who gave so much to Rosslyn Chapel, and at the "heretic" Pope who gave his blessing. We investigate the animist tradition of the chapel's carvings; the hidden history of the gospel writer St Matthew; the date of dedication of the chapel and its links with an entirely Jewish concept – the holy Shekinah. In addition we explore the chapel's links with the alternative early Christian tradition of John the Baptist and his followers, the Ebionites; their influence on the region of Champagne; on groups such as the Cistercians and Knights Templar and, in turn, Ebionite influence on Europe, Scotland, and particularly the Sinclair family.

We also offer arguments for seeing the origins of the Freemasonry in William Sinclair's need for a workforce that could keep secrets. Our discoveries regarding the astronomical alignments of the chapel add weight to our ultimate conclusions and put beyond credibility the idea that here is nothing more than a run-of-the-mill collegiate church. The existence of the light box alone shows a mastery of astronomy allied to architecture that sets Rosslyn Chapel apart from any of its contemporary structures. For the first time we are able to show that this 15th century building is not simply a place of worship, it is an observatory.

In summary, Rosslyn Chapel expresses the surviving beliefs of a form of Judaic Christianity that flourished first in and around Jerusalem during the first century AD. The people who espoused this belief thought of themselves as the direct legatees of a series of priests drawn from the Jewish Davidic line. The first of these was John the Baptist. John looked towards the arrival of a Kingdom of Heaven on Earth – nothing short of a New Jerusalem. His core beliefs were adherence to the natural laws of God, rightness of action, humility, fairness, charity and equality. It was believed that he drew his authority and inspiration from God, brought to Earth by the Shekinah and made manifest in the priests of the new but nevertheless entirely Jewish sect. The followers of this doctrine were known as Ebionites.

The Ebionites also believed that at his death John the Baptist handed the leadership of the sect to Jesus, taken on subsequently by Jesus' brother, James. After Jesus' own death a very Romanised Jew, Saul (St Paul) hijacked the story of Jesus, elevating Jesus to a unique rank that neither John nor his original followers ever intended. In popular tradition Jesus became confused with Mithras, a deity already popular in the Roman world. What ultimately followed was a form of Christianity very different to that of the Ebionites. Theirs had been a belief that enshrined the equality of all mankind, and they held that nothing earthly stood between the individual communicating with his God; neither King nor Pope.

After the Jewish Uprising of 70 AD the Jewish population of Palestine, including the Jerusalem Church of the Ebionites, was dispersed across what is now the Middle East and Europe. In small pockets it survived, as far east as Iraq and as far west as France.

In France, in the face of a jealous and often vicious Catholic Church hierarchy the core beliefs of the Ebionites were passed from parent to child across centuries. The families in question either already possessed or else absorbed Kabalistic ideas and they retained a special reverence for the Temple in Jerusalem, where they believed the heart of their religious message lay. They followed the Noahide laws and in a way they remained Jewish. Nevertheless, Ebionites in Europe married into Christian families from Frankish times onwards and they eventually gained sufficient influence to control and rule the region of Champagne. Other groups of Ebionites had settled in nearby Normandy and some of these, including the Sinclairs (meaning "Priests of the Holy Light") travelled after the Norman Conquest to England and Scotland.

Determined to see the true and original form of Christianity eclipse the feudal and oppressive Roman Christianity, the Ebionites in Champagne embarked on a series of actions (in particular the first crusade) that would regain for them the sacred city of Jerusalem, where they could re-establish their Church at its natural centre, rather than the relatively late usurpation of Rome. Their "storm-troopers" were the Knights Templar, who, as Ebionites, revered John the Baptist rather than Jesus. The political machinations that followed proved to be too great, and though the Ebionites did much to alter the fabric of Church and State in Europe, they soon lost control of Jerusalem once again.

Retrenching, the Ebionites survived in the very heart of medieval society, from where they continued to have a dramatic bearing on the development of Europe. By the 15th century Humanism began to flourish in Italy and Catholic rigidity relaxed at the highest levels. For a brief but bright time it flourished in the hearts and teachings of three crucial popes, at least one of whom, Pius II, may well have been an Ebionite himself. He was closely tied to the Sinclairs in Scotland, who bought up his illegitimate son, and this remarkable Pope even attempted to resurrect the by now destroyed Templars in a different form.

Crucial to our argument is the figure of Sir Gilbert Haye, one of the most educated and enlightened Scots of his day, who had spent two and a half decades in France. In addition he travelled extensively, collecting manuscripts and knowledge, meeting with the men whose enlightened ideas and actions would kick-start the Renaissance. He worked hard towards the day when he could return to his homeland, to help construct the new Temple that would rise far from Jerusalem. In 1456 Gilbert arrived in Rosslyn and work on the chapel commenced above ground.

Rosslyn Chapel was specifically built with the first and second Temples of Jerusalem in mind but it also had to serve the purposes of a Christian church. The chapel was dedicated to St Matthew and we are the first authors to show why this was the case and how significant the fact was to those who built the Chapel and to the Ebionites as a whole. The Hebrew Gospel of St Matthew was close to their heart because it eulogised John the Baptist and demonstrated that he had preceded Jesus as head of the Jerusalem sect. St Matthew was also important because his feast day falls on 21 September, a date which also marks the Autumn Equinox and which stands at the heart of Rosslyn Chapel's position as a celestial observatory.

The choice of the pivotal period in September for the Feast Day of the chapel was crucial. Not least it coincided with the Jewish New Year and was also the time at which both the first and second Temples in Jerusalem had been dedicated. It also lay at the heart of the old Mystery religions such as that of Demeter and it occurred when the sun occupied the zodiac sign of Virgo, which was itself equated with the Shekinah, a mystical symbol of great significance to Jews and Christians alike.

Rosslyn Chapel was built to the most exacting standards and designed so that twice a year, at the time of the Spring and Autumn Equinox, light from the sun would flood directly into the chapel through the specially created light box, acting as a sign that the Holy Shekinah was resident in the building, seasonally fulfilling through nature the ancient, sacred covenant between God and Mankind.

Of course it is possible to read the Chapel in purely orthodox Christian terms. It is equally possible to see it as representing topical, 15th century philosophical imperatives. Many of the carvings are associated with Sir Gilbert Hayes writings, such as *Alexander's Journey to Paradise*, a book of natural philosophy. Other carvings point to the *Secretum Secretorum*, a book specifically written to give advice to princes about how to live their lives and to govern their subjects with fairness, chivalry and honesty. Equally, the many Green Men carved into the stone of the Chapel and the abundant foliage could be equated to the moralistic tale of *Sir Gawain and the Green Knight*. But to the initiate who truly understood its significance Rosslyn Chapel remained a Jewish/Christian temple that contained within it the all-important Tree of Life, a symbol that was found in all known religions of the period.

The conclusion we have reached is that Rosslyn Chapel is, first and foremost, a monument to tolerance and understanding. It is a legacy from a group of people who have shown immense patience and fortitude and whose greatest contribution was their unyielding belief that God is available to all and unique to none. It speaks of individuality and liberty, yet it was built well before the appearance of the Age of Reason and even before the first flush of the dawn of Renaissance was starting to light up the far distant shores of Northern Italy. The ideas behind it are radical for their time, though surprisingly relevant for today. Ironically they found their expression just a few years before the age of print, not in words but in one of the most dedicated examples of the medieval stonemason's craft ever undertaken. Understanding what Rosslyn Chapel means will enable us to look afresh at the conventional story of the development of Europe and the opening of new worlds. It will also lead us to a new understanding of what a revitalised Christianity could mean for today. We have come to see it as one of the most important buildings in Europe, if not the world. The reason its message has been lost for half a millennium is that the window of opportunity it offered was closed when the Reformation, followed by the Counter Reformation, introduced a new, hard and polarised dogmatism into European religious affairs.

This in turn led to the religious wars of the 16th and 17th centuries, some of the most deadly struggles Europe has ever experienced. In an age during which wars of religion are becoming common again, and when fanatical beliefs lead to unquestionable horrors, we look towards the ultimately simple message of Rosslyn Chapel, in which entrenched values are replaced by intellectual curiosity and common myth, and specific dogma gives way to universal truth. We hope that in some small way our findings regarding this amazing structure will build on the much-needed recognition that, above all personal and racial differences, the human spirit endures and that it carries a simple and unbending truth about the Godhead; because, as an inscription carved into Rosslyn Chapel over five hundred years ago tells us: The truth is strongest of all.

1

A confection in stone

I F FIRST IMPRESSIONS count, it is a near miracle that Rosslyn Chapel has now become so famous that literally hundreds of thousands of people pass through its entrance each year. The road to the village of Rosslyn, though as picturesque as any in this part of Scotland, is not exciting. The village of Roslin, so rurally inviting, is now a tiny village compared with the splendid Georgian capital Edinburgh only 6 miles away, but this was not always so.

As far as the chapel itself is concerned, if you are expecting to be confronted by something on the scale of Notre Dame in Paris or Westminster Abbey in London, forget it. Rosslyn Chapel itself does not even rank a place of honour on the main street of the village. It is approached by way of something that until very recently could only have been described as a muddy track. The building is small in size, squat in nature and dark, perhaps even slightly foreboding, in appearance.

At the time of writing these words Rosslyn Chapel glowers out from under a huge steel canopy, erected over the building because of problems in the masonry. Captured by this modern monstrosity, essential as it might be to the well-being of the building, the chapel looks even smaller than is really the case. Unlike many other British churches it has no tower or spire and its exterior carvings, of which there are many, are virtually invisible

Rosslyn Chapel in 1917 (Courtesy of Peter Stubbs, Edinburgh)
Inset: Artist's impression of what Rosslyn Chapel may have looked like in its totally finished state

under the grime of ages and have suffered significantly as a result of the sort of weather that Scotland expects on an almost daily basis.

It might not seem like a promising start but we have yet to meet anyone who left Rosslyn Chapel without having been moved, mystified and even mesmerised by the experience.

Generally speaking visitors have been primed about the chapel and so are keen to see its interior immediately. Any real search around the exterior is usually left until last and that is probably sensible because it takes time for one's eyes to become accustomed to the intricacies of the medieval stonemason's art. This is appreciated much more within the chapel, where most of the carvings are still crisp and clean.

What greets each visitor as they walk in through the southern door is little short of breathtaking. At first sight it seems as though almost every square inch of available wall space is occupied with carvings of one sort or another – in fact there are so many that the effect is giddying, leaving one stunned and unable to see any appreciable point of entry to such a series of stories frozen in stone.

There is a natural tendency to walk immediately to the eastern end of the chapel, to where the altar table stands. It is a plain affair, like a digestive biscuit surrounded by rich cream cakes and as such is generally ignored by eyes that are drawn to the sumptuously carved pillars, window surrounds, arches, bosses and friezes. It is at this point that different personal interests become apparent. Those who are of a Freemasonic bent will immediately walk towards the so-called Apprentice Pillar, on the north side of the altar. Its barley-twist design is striking but the dragons around its base often go unnoticed. People who are drawn to the naturalistic and even pagan qualities of some of the carvings will begin to look for the Green Men who peer down from the most unlikely places, making a search for them a rewarding delight.

Partly because the place is usually so busy these days there isn't really time to do any more than sip at the fountain of possibilities that exists in every nook and cranny. 'Here' there are amusing little depictions of men playing bagpipes; whilst 'there' are ancient, horned kings, figures from the Old Testament of the Bible, floriate designs with leaves and buds, branches heavy with fruit and vegetables, birds, animals and puzzling geometric shapes.

Lifting one's eyes towards the ceiling they receive yet another assault as the arched roof gives up its mass of flower designs and, towards the back

The Chapel's wonderful carvings

Stars carved onto the roof of the Chapel

Rosslyn Chapel from Rosslyn Glen, showing the elevated nature of the Chapel

of the chapel, a veritable universe of stars. By now the senses are reeling but the most mysterious part of the building is still to be explored.

To the right of the altar there is a flight of steep stone steps, the treads of which have become slightly dangerous with the footfall of ages. The journey down into the crypt is not for the faint-hearted. Even here there are carvings, some of them bearing traces of colour, giving only a slight indication of what the chapel must have looked like when all the stonework was replete with bright hues and the carvings leapt out in 3D reality.

On the wall to the left at the bottom of the staircase are strange designs pecked out on the stone of the wall itself – a masonry sketchbook used by those who created this incongruous masterpiece nearly six hundred years ago. To the right are a couple of small rooms, now used as storage areas but further on to the left is a recess that though plain and damp is just as exciting to many as the chapel itself. The wall to the left of this recess marks the place of access to the crypt proper. These days it is just a solid wall but to most people it is the unknown contents of this subterranean vault that have a significant and abiding appeal. What is to be found behind these great stones? Is it the massed ranks of the Sinclair Lords, still wearing their battle armour, sleeping their way through Scotland's great resurgence and oblivious in death to the fame of their name and titles across the world? If we were to remove the wall would we find a Freemasonic temple, the Ark of the Covenant, mountains of gold, the Holy Grail or even, as has been suggested, the head of Jesus? The sense of wonder and frustration is almost unbearable.

Back out in the fresh air one begins to look with new eyes at the exterior of the building. The steel shroud around the chapel might be hideous but it does have one advantage. It allows access, by way of a series of stairs, to the roof. Walking along this gantry it is possible to see that the same stonemasons who lavished so much time on the interior carvings gave no less attention to the ornamentation of spires and gargoyles that would be virtually invisible from the ground.

Around the north side of the chapel, the view from the gantry allows a glimpse of the ruins of Rosslyn Castle, not too far distant. The land falls away steeply to the east and all around is an avalanche of trees, tumbling billows of green upon which the chapel must have once ridden like an ornate galleon.

One visit is rarely enough and how frustrating it must be, especially from a position at the other side of the world, to look back at one's photographs and guide books and to realise that no matter how intent the gaze, it had only been possible to take in a tiny fraction of the medieval delights contained within this small space. Second visits tend to be more circumspect but in their way just as frustrating. It's hard to concentrate and one is bombarded with snatches of conversation from other visitors because summer and winter alike this place is rarely quiet. Names such as that of Dan Brown, Knight and Lomas, Wallace-Murphy and others are whispered in every corner and it becomes obvious there here is a six-century old box of delights that has been so pawed over, so analysed and explored that it must now rank as one of the most famous buildings in the world.

Herein lies the problem. Rosslyn Chapel is not simply one old building. It is the starting point of numerous adventures, each of which sees a different chapel and an alternative explanation for its incongruous existence. Is it really an exact scale model copy of Solomon's Temple in far-off Jerusalem? Was it created as a glorification of the little understood pseudo-religion that is Freemasonry or might it be a lasting memorial to the famed Knights Templar of old, who carved a military and economic path through the feudal landscape of the whole known world of their day?

Perhaps we need a starting point. Whatever Rosslyn Chapel is actually meant to represent it surely is as far from being a run-of-the-mill church as Harrods is from being a village shop. With no insult intended to those worshipers who gather here on Sundays or at the stations of the Christian Year, Rosslyn Chapel might be 'used' as a church (and it is certain that it was called such by those who dreamed up this confection in stone) but it clearly was and is also much more than a normal place of worship.

Legends associating Rosslyn Chapel with Freemasonry abound. The most famous of these is with regard to the Apprentice Pillar, the most ornate and incredible piece of carving in the whole building. (A picture of the pillar can be seen in the colour section.) The Apprentice Pillar stands adjacent to the altar. There is a Masonic story that says that a Master Mason who had been chosen to carve the ornate pillar for this location refused to do so until he had travelled to Rome, presumably to gain divine inspiration for the task. Whilst he was absent his apprentice had a dream, in which he saw the finished pillar in all its glory. The apprentice set to work and by the time his Master had returned, the pillar as we see it today was finished. The Master Mason was so enraged that he picked up his mallet and struck the lad so hard on the head he was killed instantly.

This may be an interesting story but that is all it turns out to be: there is no historical record of such an event ever taking place. It seems likely that

Freemasons, having already decided that the chapel was sacred to their Craft, invented the story to fit the existence of the pillar. Scottish Rite Freemasonry, as far as its historical records are concerned, does not predate Rosslyn Chapel and the place may have been significant to the Craft since its creation. But this does not mean the chapel was 'built' with Freemasonry in mind.

Dragons carved at the base of the Princes Pillar

Rosslyn Chapel is also considered by many to have been created by members of a religious order known as the Poor Knights of Christ and the Temple of Solomon. These men were and are more usually known as the Knights Templar. But the Knights Templar were destroyed in 1307, well over a hundred years before Rosslyn Chapel was planned or created. It is possible that those responsible for the chapel considered themselves to be associated with the Templars. It's a long stretch to claim that Rosslyn Chapel was planned and built by an order of fighting monks that didn't even exist at the time.

The head of the so-called Apprentice. The head has been carelessly divested of its beard at some time to make it look younger

Back in the 1990s Christopher Knight and Robert Lomas wrote the bestselling book *The Hiram Key*, an attempt to establish what Freemasonry was really all about. Knight and Lomas ultimately demonstrated a connection between the Knights Templars and the rise of Freemasonry and suggested that Rosslyn Chapel was associated with both organisations.[1] They further speculated that what the chapel really represented was a scale model copy of the original Temple of Solomon, which once stood on the

---

1 See Appendix 1 for a full description of the Knights Templar and Appendix 2 for an explanation of Freemasonry.

Temple Mound in Jerusalem. They maintained that existent Masonic ritual demonstrates that the founders of the Knights Templar had conducted a dig on the Temple Mound during the 12th century, and that there they had discovered the ruins of the original temple. The suggestion is that Rosslyn was built to house all or part of the treasures uncovered by the Templars and removed to Europe for safety. This they estimate would be found in a vault far below the chapel. This is an example of a story about the Chapel we initially approached with scepticism, but came to seem more likely in the context of our discoveries.

On the other side of the divide we have those who maintain that Rosslyn Chapel is simply what history says it is. Back in the 15th century a powerful Earl by the name of William Sinclair decided to glorify his name, as did many men of his rank and station, by building what was intended eventually to be a large collegiate church. Rosslyn Chapel is merely the 'Lady Chapel' of something that was meant to be far bigger, but the family was either strapped for funds or simply lost interest in the project.

So which is it? Our twelve-year co-operation has resulted in this book. The reason we are so confident about our findings is that they are based upon historical records, and because we have looked very closely at the lives of the men who were most responsible for the chapel's existence.

We will show a Rosslyn Chapel that has never been seen before. Between the sterile pages of orthodox history and the world of fantasy lies a story that is both compelling and honest.

2

The Chapel and its decoration

ROSSLYN CHAPEL IS built in the Gothic style. This method of building, which dates from the 12th century, is typified by its use of rounded but pointed-topped arches, properly known as ogives. The development of the Gothic style was a significant advance over the older Romanesque because it coped with the great loads of stone buildings in a new and revolutionary way. Gravitational forces were transferred to the outside of the building where they were dissipated with the use of flying buttresses, allowing for thinner walls and greater window space.

In most Gothic buildings the ogives generally spread the load of roofs too but Rosslyn Chapel does not rely on the forest of ribs to be seen in other Gothic buildings. It has a barrel-vaulted roof that runs along its length and outside the forces created are transferred to the pinnacles that support the flying buttresses. There are 32 different varieties of arch in the chapel, which is stunning considering the size of the building. This is only one respect in which the interested visitor might get the impression that the chapel's architects and builders were 'showing off'.

Rosslyn Chapel contains such a vast array of stone carvings, both inside and out, that the overall effect is confusing and apparently abstract. However, the chapel does contain a number of very definite themes. Very few of these are unique to this building, as for example with representations

A typical Gothic arched window in the Chapel

of the Green Man or depictions of angels and foliate designs, all of which are to be seen elsewhere. The real puzzle in the case of Rosslyn Chapel is not that these carvings are present but rather lies in the sheer number of examples on display.

The Green Man

One of the greatest games amongst visitors to Rosslyn Chapel, and especially for children, is to spot as many Green Men as possible whilst wandering around both the interior and exterior of the building. At the last estimate there are thought to be in the region of 110 examples of the Green Man inside and outside the chapel but as John keeps discovering, this is hardly likely to be the actual total. Many are located in hard-to-find nooks and crannies and some of those on the exterior of the building are so worn as to be almost impossible to see.

The first and most important question with regard to these particular carvings has to be; what is the Green Man? This turns out to be a far more complicated question than might at first seem to be the case. Representations of the Green Man, even within Rosslyn Chapel, vary considerably but generally speaking the term, which was first coined by Lady Raglan as recently as 1939, refers to a male face that either peers out between branches or leaves, has tendrils emanating from its mouth, eyes, nose or ears, or which is composed in part or in whole of foliage.

Versions of the Green Man are found as far away as Malaysia, India, the Middle and Near East and in many places throughout Italy. He was popular in Roman times and appears to have been adopted in the decoration of Christian churches from an early period. In truth the Green Man is probably as old as humanity, but this realisation still falls far short of explaining what he actually 'is' or 'represents'.

One of the best explanations for the existence of the Green Man is that he originates in what is most certainly one of humanity's earliest religious responses – Animism.

Our first true human ancestors gained something that their earlier animal counterparts did not have – they possessed cognitive awareness. The cleverest apes can count, recognise objects, have a fairly good memory and even use tools but there is some doubt about their actual 'awareness' of their own existence, as differentiated from every other ape and the world at large. When the first human being was able to say, or more probably to think, 'I am', he separated himself from the rest of creation. He was able to look at the world in a different way. In the absence of scientific understanding he observed the movement of a cloud, the flames of a volcano or the rapid growth of plants in the spring and he wondered – in a way that his ape counterpart never could. There just had to be an explanation, rational or not, to the various processes that took place in the world and early man seems to have come to the understandable conclusion (in the absence of any other evidence) that everything was imbued with its own force of spirit.

It would be a very long road to the acceptance of a single deity to explain everything that went on in the world; good, bad or indifferent. It would be even longer before humanity could see how the natural forces of physics could bring about such mystifying happenings, and so to a more primitive mind every tree, each stream and in particular every electrical storm quite clearly had its own internal motivation. It wasn't far from this to a

A typical representation of the Green Man

realisation that it might be best to stay on the right side of these other 'entities', and so worship of one sort or another began.

The Green Man may well be a hangover of this form of Animism. He represents the 'spirit' of growing nature and comes from a period when much of the world, and in particular Europe, was covered in trees. How many of us can remember from childhood the sheer panic of looking at a gnarled old oak on the edge of a dark wood and seeing in its twisted branches the form of a living, breathing monster?

From hunter-gatherers, whose home and living was partly in the forest, amongst the 'tree creatures' that undoubtedly dwelled there, we eventually gravitated to farming. We cleared the huge stands of trees but it seems we

Jack in the Green from Rosslyn Chapel, linked to Cernunnos

never quite forgot our sense of wonder and awe regarding the unknown inhabitants of that dark and often impenetrable world.

As far as Britain in concerned there was an explosion of Green Man carvings within Christian churches that began from around the early 12th century. In the vast majority of cases representations of the Green Man are tucked away in inaccessible corners. He is often to be found carved onto the underside of misericords. These are also known as 'mercy seats' and are found in the choir stalls of ancient parish churches, minsters and cathedrals. Misericords are not so much seats as small hinged shelves on which members of the choir could perch themselves during long services. Representations of the Green Man are often to be found on the bottom of these hinged shelves and are often very beautifully carved.

The Green Man is also to be found carved onto roof bosses or tucked into the bottom edge of arches but he is usually difficult to find and one gets the impression that his presence was frowned upon by the Church authorities. Or it may be the case that 'hunting the Green Man' was always something of a game, even during medieval times, though this seems an inadequate explanation for the amount of work that went into carving them.

Rarely does any particular church boast more than one or two examples of the Green Man but there are exceptions apart from Rosslyn Chapel. One of the best is the Chapter House at Southwell Minster (now Southwell Cathedral) in Nottinghamshire, England. The Chapter House at Southwell dates back to the 13th century and was completed in 1286. Here the Green Man is brought to an obvious and deliberate art form and certainly is not hidden away. Each of the Green Men in the Chapter House at Southwell has a unique face and the leaves that adorn the faces are different in each case, reflecting one of the species of plant to be found in the district at the time the Chapter House was built.

Interestingly enough Southwell, like Rosslyn Chapel, was a collegiate church, one of the greatest and most powerful of the collegiate churches of Britain. This may be a coincidence but there could be a connection, if only because collegiate churches were so much more autonomous than normal parish churches and so could probably push the bounds of the acceptable as far as church decoration was concerned.

With his ancient origins and his association with fertility and the changing seasons, the Green Man is representative of deities from cultures that inhabited Europe long before the rise of Christianity. Some historians equate him with a Celtic deity called Cernunnos. Cernunnos was worshiped extensively in pre-Roman Gaul and also in Britain. He was a stag-headed god. His worshipers believed he was born annually at the time of the Winter Solstice (21 December) and that in the spring he married the goddess Beltane, before dying at the time of the Autumn Equinox (21 September). In this form Cernunnos is representative of a god who appears in most early religions and who is often referred to as 'the corn god'. The corn god has many guises and appears in increasingly more complex circumstances as patterns of mythology and religion across the world became more sophisticated. However, his original characteristics are always obvious. The corn god represents the tangible face of nature. Nowhere is he better described than in the case of the dying and reborn god of a people who inhabited the Island of Crete as early as 2,000 BC. These people, who represented Europe's first super-civilization, are known to us as the 'Minoans'. They enjoyed a sophisticated society but appear to have maintained a religious imperative that was probable endemic to most of Europe and Asia by the time of the late Stone Age.

To the Minoans there was only one enduring and perpetual deity. This was the Great Goddess, a personification of the Earth and nature. Superimposed onto the constant presence of the Goddess was her consort, the God. He appeared in two forms, as the Young God and the Old God. In a yearly dance that seems to have lain at the heart of Minoan religion, the Goddess gave birth to a son, who was worshiped as the 'Young God'. As the year advanced the Young God gradually grew older, until he became the consort of the Goddess and coupled with her. By now he was the Old God, and he had to die so that his counterpart and son the Young God could once again be born to the world.

This belief pattern is a direct reflection of the seasonal quality of nature. In the autumn plants die back after setting seed, only to reappear in the spring as fresh, new shoots that gradually mature throughout the summer. This was especially important to farmers and is why the Young God of Minoan legend came to be known in many religions as the 'Corn God'. A wonderful old British folk song shows this belief encapsulated in story form long after the advent of Christianity. It is called John Barleycorn. In a typical version the lyrics are as follows:

There was three men came out of the west,
Their fortunes for to try,
And these three men made a solemn vow,
John Barleycorn should die.
They ploughed, they sowed, they harrowed him in,
Throwed clods upon his head,
And these three man made a solemn vow,
John Barleycorn was dead.

Then they let him lie for a very long time
Till the rain from heaven did fall,
Then little Sir John sprung up his head,
And soon amazed them all.
They let him stand till midsummer
Till he looked both pale and wan,
And little Sir John he growed a long beard
And so became a man.

They hired men with the scythes so sharp
To cut him off at the knee,
They rolled him and tied him by the waist,
And served him most barbarously.
They hired men with the sharp pitchforks
Who pricked him to the heart,
And the loader he served him worse than that,
For he bound him to the cart.

They wheeled him round and round the field
Till they came unto a barn,
And there they made a solemn mow
of poor John Barleycorn.
They hired men with the crab-tree sticks
To cut him skin from bone,
And the miller he served him worse than that,
For he ground him between two stones.

Here's little Sir John in a nut-brown bowl,
And brandy in a glass;
And little Sir John in the nut-brown bowl
Proved the stronger man at last.
And the huntsman he can't hunt the fox,
Nor so loudly blow his horn,
And the tinker he can't mend kettles or pots
Without a little of Barleycorn.

In this example the Corn God is related to a specific cereal crop, barley, which in medieval times was the chief ingredient of beer.

The song offers an example of the way the Corn God has been viewed across many thousands of years. To the vast majority of early farmers in Europe and Asia the conjoining of God and Goddess was essential to the continuation of nature and to the husbandry of plants that sustained humanity. A consequence of this was the annual death of the God.

As religions became more advanced, so the Corn God gained a more complicated biography and a wealth of different names, but across countless cultures the sacrificial nature of his existence was not forgotten.

To the Ancient Egyptians he was Osiris, who was killed and eventually torn to pieces by a rival god. However, his adoring wife Isis, herself simply a counterpart of the old Great Goddess, found the pieces of his body and brought them together again, at the same time inseminating herself with his phallus.

To the Greeks the Corn God eventually became Dionysus, another character who, like John Barleycorn, was set upon by brigands who killed him, roasted his body and consumed it. Nevertheless Dionysus was born again, thanks to the intervention of the Greek version of the Great Goddess, Demeter.

Neither was the sacrificial nature of the Corn God forgotten, even when there was a pivotal change in religion that saw the old Great Goddess deposed in favour of powerful masculine deities. One of the most important deities of Roman times was Mithras, who was especially important to Government officials and to members of the Roman army. Mithras, like Osiris and Dionysus, was killed and ultimately resurrected, and many of his characteristics passed to Christianity, becoming entwined in the story of Jesus.

As one of the most recent of the sacrificed gods, Jesus shows all the characteristics of his earlier counterparts. He, or those who manipulated his biography after the event, left no doubt about his association with the old Corn God. Immediately before his crucifixion Jesus held a meal with his disciples, which is known as the Last Supper[2]. These are the words spoken by Jesus at that time or at least his words according to the Gospel writers:

While they were eating, Jesus took bread, gave thanks and broke it, and gave it to his disciples, saying, 'Take it; this is my body.'

Immediately after this, in Mark 14:23 and 24 we read:

And he took a cup, and when he had given thanks he gave it to them, and they all drank of it.
And he said to them, 'This is my blood of the covenant, which is poured out for many.'

---

2 *The Virgin and the Pentacle*, Alan Butler, O Books, London, 2006

There could hardly be a better example of a man equating himself with the Corn God of old than this. Of course we have no way of knowing if these were the actual words spoken by Jesus at the time, but whether they are or not, they have become the focus of the Christian Communion, undoubtedly the most celebrated Mystery of the Christian Church to this day.

In addition to the animistic qualities of the Green Man, it may be that Christian iconographers equated the sacrificial nature of the Green Man with that of the Christian story. One cannot help thinking that this would be the story told to any inquiring member of the Church hierarchy that visited Green Man rich buildings such as Southwell Minster and Rosslyn Chapel.

Gods of the wood

Cernunnos, the old Celtic horned god of the woods was certainly not forgotten by medieval times. He has a well-known counterpart whose most common name is Herne the Hunter. Like Cernunnos Herne has a long beard and the horns of a young stag. Even his name has an older origin because in popular use the name Cernunnos became 'Cerne', which eventually came to be spoken as 'Herne'.

The sacrificial nature of characters associated with the Green Man were popular in other story cycles that were already prevalent at the time Rosslyn Chapel was being completed. In particular we find these in the legends of King Arthur, which had been present in British folklore from a very early period but were especially popular from the 12th century. It was at this time that Geoffrey of Monmouth wrote his fictional *Historia Regum Britanniae*.

King Arthur was probably a real character, most likely a 6th century leader of the combined Celtic tribes that struggled against the forces of the Anglo Saxons, who launched invasions against Britain after the withdrawal of the Roman legions. Although almost certainly never actually a king, Arthur became a central character in legend and the real man probably became associated with earlier legends of demi-gods and heroes from Celtic mythology. Gradually, more and more works associated with King Arthur and his mythical knights of the round table appeared, not just in Britain but also in France, and his popularity shone like a star throughout the medieval period.

The central theme of many of the stories from the King Arthur legends deals with a search for the Holy Grail, the vessel from which Jesus was said to have drunk at the Last Supper. In the stories many of Arthur's knights die in the quest to discover the Holy Grail, and there are clearly ancient themes at work that relate directly to the sacrificial nature of gods and heroes from much earlier mythologies. In the story *Sir Gawain and the Green Knight* for example, the Green Knight seems to embody the characteristics of the Green Man. In this story Sir Gawain accepts a challenge from the mysterious Green Knight on New Year's Day at Camelot.

The Green Knight allows Sir Gawain to take one blow at him with a battle axe, on the understanding that Gawain will travel to the 'Green Chapel' one year and one day later so that the Green Knight can return the blow. Sir Gawain cuts off the head of the Green Knight but instead of dying the Green Knight picks up his head and retires from Camelot. Sir Gawain dutifully travels to the Green Chapel at the appointed date but is entertained for three days prior to the contest by a local lord, whose wife tries on three occasions to seduce Sir Gawain. On each occasion he maintains his chastity and offers only a kiss in the face of her advances.

On the appointed day Sir Gawain visits the Green Chapel and there meets the Green Knight. His adversary takes not one but three strikes at Sir Gawain but he suffers no more than a cut to his neck. He received this wound only because he had been given a green girdle by the lord's wife. This token he had kept and failed to report to the Lord.

The moral of the story seems to be that virtue is its own reward, and *Sir Gawain and the Green Knight* is typical of the romances of King Arthur. However, it might be from an even older and more exotic source. In the Islamic Holy Book, the Qur'an, there is a story about a virtuous knight by the name of Al-Khidr, which literally means 'Green Man'. Al-Khidr is tested three times by Moses, and proves himself to be ultimately virtuous, even though his responses to Moses appear to be evil. It is possible that something of *Sir Gawain and the Green Knight* came to Britain at the time of the Crusades and became enmeshed in a different form in the Arthurian romances. The story of *Sir Gawain and the Green Knight* first appears in a written form in the 14th century.

Is there a direct connection between *Sir Gawain and the Green Knight* and the Rosslyn Chapel? It has to be remembered that when it was completed the Chapel would have looked very different than it does today. Not only were the sumptuous carvings superbly created but the art of the stone carver was enhanced by that of the painter. Most if not all of the carved stone of Rosslyn Chapel would have been brightly coloured and the impression to anyone entering the building for the first time must have been breathtaking. Bearing in mind the amount of carved foliage, together with all the examples of the Green Man present, one could almost certainly be forgiven for calling Rosslyn Chapel the 'Green Chapel', which is the place where Sir Gawain met the Green Knight in order to receive the promised blow. The story of *Sir Gawain and the Green Knight* was already in circulation and popular by the time Rosslyn Chapel was planned and executed, and it isn't beyond the realms of possibility that both Sir Gilbert Haye and Earl William Sinclair, the Chapel's creators, were familiar with the story and equated it with their own masterpiece. There are also strong similarities between the countryside described in *Sir Gawain and the Green Knight* and that surrounding Rosslyn Chapel

Whoever wrote *Sir Gawain and the Green Knight* talks of deeply wooded valleys replete with oak, a castle on a promontory and the fact that the Green Chapel itself was built on a grassy mound. It all sounds uncannily like the area around Rosslyn Castle and Rosslyn Chapel. We do not suggest that the story was written with Rosslyn Chapel in mind, because it predates the chapel. It has to be a possibility though that those who planned and built the chapel were aware of the striking similarities. The stories regarding King Arthur and his court were extremely popular by the 15th century and represented one of very few departures from books that were almost inevitably dry tomes or religious works.

Interestingly enough there is an aspect of the Green Man as he is seen within Rosslyn Chapel that as far as we can ascertain is unique. Some years ago John began to study and photograph the Green Men throughout the chapel and realised that they look very different on the four walls of the chapel.

He saw that the depictions of the Green Man carved onto the walls, arches and bosses at the east end are all young looking, impish, mischievous and filled with vigour. Moving round to the south wall we find a more mature looking series of Green Man depictions. On the west wall of the Chapel depictions of the Green Man look older still. The faces are contorted and the expressions are somehow forlorn and careworn. They

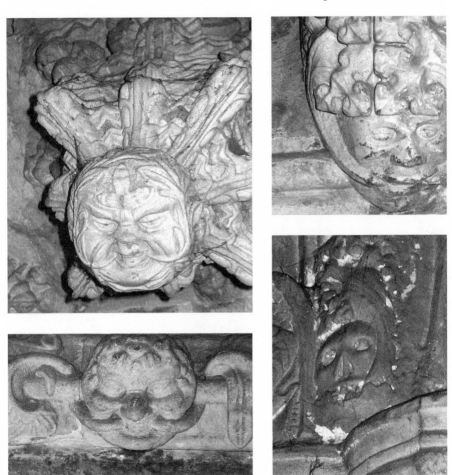

The changing face of the Green Man in Rosslyn Chapel, from luxuriant spring to gaunt and skull-like winter

The very rare Green Woman of Rosslyn Chapel

are also surrounded by less foliage. Finally, on the north wall of the chapel we find the most striking change of all. There are Green Men present but the majority of them are represented as skulls. The branches and tendrils of plants are still present but they are generally devoid of foliage and the general impression is one of death and decay. The message being put across to those who look at the chapel closely is that life is closely tied to nature and to the passing of the seasons.

Rosslyn Chapel is also unusual in that it contains at least one example of a Green Woman. These are very rare. The face that is undeniably female is to be found to the right of the altar, guarding the wall that separated the chapel proper from the entrance to the crypt. She is within that part of the chapel that has always been known as the 'Lady Altar' and it is possible that this position originally represented the only genuine altar to be found above ground level in Rosslyn Chapel.

The chapel is also replete with carvings of angels, and in fact there are more angels than Green Men. Most of the angels are very beautifully carved and often have exotic hairstyles. Some carry books, others scrolls, and they are to be seen at almost every turn, though they proliferate at the east end of the chapel, where the carving is at its most lavish.

The angels

Angels are of course common in church decoration, but they are represented at their best and most complex within Rosslyn Chapel. In both Judaism and Christianity angels represent the emissaries between God and man. The word angel is specifically mentioned 108 times in the Old Testament of the Bible and 175 times in the New Testament. Neither are angels restricted to Judaeo Christian traditions. Such entities were talked and written about in Sumerian and Babylonian times and it is probably from this source that they found their way into Judaism, and ultimately Christianity.

There are different spheres or types of angel, each with its own designated role to play in Creation. Within Judaism and Christianity there are said to be innumerable angels, but not all of them are good. Satan, who himself was once one of the archangels, fell from the grace of God and has his own attendant angels, closely matching the heavenly variety. Examples of

Exquisite carvings of angels from Rosslyn Chapel

both good and bad angels are to be seen in Rosslyn Chapel and doubtless all of them tell a specific story, but their true meaning hints at something far beyond the role angels play in Judaic or Christian literature and, as we shall see, their presence lies at the heart of the esoteric story the Chapel tells.

Vegetation

The other major theme within the chapel is the constant stone reference to nature – a positive paradise of trees, plants, tendrils, foliage, flowers and fruit. All of the vegetation emanates from the top of the pillar variously known as the Apprentice Pillar and the Princes Pillar, which is the extreme right-hand pillar in the chapel when looking east. From the dragons at its base carved vines twist around the Princes pillar and explode into innumerable species. Present in the chapel, and extending around much of its wall space, there are representations of indigenous plants and members of species such as aloe and maize that, by the dictates of orthodox history, should not be there at all.

In addition to apples, pears and various types of soft fruit that would have been common to Britain in the 15th century, the carvings also show citrus fruit and pomegranates – which the average individual in Scotland at the time would probably never have seen.

Superbly detailed carving of foliage

Perhaps dozens of different species of flowers can be seen around the chapel walls, many of which, such as the common dog rose and the lily can be easily identified. There are flowers of the daisy family and more exotic blooms that could well be orchids, and the roof of the chapel in particular is a feast of floral designs.

For years the sheer scale of the naturalistic carvings in Rosslyn Chapel puzzled us greatly, as did the realisation that they all stemmed from the top of a single pillar. We were eventually to discover the answer to this puzzle, and there is an almost certain connection between all the carved vegetation and those enigmatic faces of the Green Man.

Culdeans

Early Scottish Christianity was of a version known as Culdean. Culdean Christianity was of a peculiarly British origin and was heavily influenced by the religion and its attendant holy men that had existed before

Christianity arrived in Britain. These priests were known as Druids, a word that ultimately means 'Oak Man'. Druidic temples existed amongst groves of trees and in forest clearings and the Druids themselves were well-trained and educated wise men, who not only preached religion but arbitrated between the tribes. Their persons were inviolate and their word law.

Early Christian monks in Britain sported the same sort of costume and the distinctive hairstyle of the Druids and they lived a very similar peripatetic existence. It may be because of the close connections between the Druids and the Celtic monks that naturalistic elements found their way to the heart of Culdean Christianity, because they clearly lay at the heart of pre-Christian British beliefs.

Although Rome had always frowned on peculiarly Culdean beliefs and practices, they were far from dead in Scotland in the 15th century. A particularly influential order of monks, originally from France, known as the Tironensians, had several major abbeys in Scotland, one of which, Kilwinning, was built on Sinclair land not far from Rosslyn. The Tironensians were, first and foremost, Culdean in their religious practices and so maintained the old reverence for nature in all its forms. In addition they were great builders – probably more so than any other Christian monastic order. They loved ornamentation and considered its creation their own peculiar form of devotion – prayers in stone. The proximity of Kilwinning and the other Tironensian abbeys to Rosslyn, together with the fact that Earl William Sinclair must have known them well, may partly explain the profusion of naturalistic images within the chapel. Put simply, the old Culdean love of nature and of growing things was as alive in Scotland in the 15th century as it had ever been, so it is not surprising that it proliferates in Rosslyn Chapel.

Towards the west end of the roof in the chapel the theme ceases to be foliate and becomes cosmological. Here there are masses of five-pointed stars, amongst which can be picked out a sun, a moon, what looks like a planet and a face that could be that of John the Baptist, Jesus or even God himself.

When we began our research on the Chapel we started by picking up the main, obvious themes of the decoration, and to look at their background. But why are the carvings so prolific and what is it they are trying to tell us? In the search for an answer the first step is to look closely at the men who were directly responsible for the chapel's creation.

3

Earl William Sinclair

THERE IS NO doubt that Rosslyn Chapel ultimately owes its existence primarily to one rich and powerful individual. His name was William Sinclair and at the time the chapel was conceived he was Earl of Orkney, Chancellor of Scotland, blood-tied to the throne of Scotland and one of the most influential men of his period.

Ancestry

William came from an illustrious and ancient family. Although not included on the commemorative roll in Battle Abbey, Hastings, it is likely that the Sinclairs first appeared in Britain at the time of the Norman Conquest. This took place in 1066 when Duke William of Normandy embarked across the English Channel with a large army and defeated the Anglo Saxons under their king Harold. One of the knights accompanying William was a man with the same Christian name, in this case William de Sancto Claro. (William of St Clair or St Clare). He may well have come from Saint-Clair-sur-Elle in Normandy. Another popular contender is a village still called St Clair, near to Pont d'Eveque, which is also in Normandy.

The name St Clair is said to come from St Clarus, a very early and semi-mythical Christian saint who is supposed to have been born in Rochester, England. Clarus travelled to the area that would one day be known as Normandy. There he lived a holy life, was martyred and subsequently canonised.

The names St Clare, and its alternative St Clair, eventually became Sinclair, and it is from these Norman knights that the whole large clan of Sinclair ultimately derives. Certainly the family must have offered significant assistance to William the Conqueror because within three generations their name was to be found associated with a significant number of English counties and they also had a strong presence in Wales as well as Scotland.

It was during the reign of King David I (1124-1153) that the Barony of Roslin was established, the first such Baron being another William St Clair or Sinclair, this one nicknamed 'the seemly'. William the Seemly died fighting his erstwhile ally William the Conqueror, by now King William I of England, when the king marched north to fight the Scots not long after his conquest of England.

The Sinclairs are also historically associated with a character known as 'Edgar the Atheling'. Edgar was a great grandson of an earlier English King called Ethelred the Unready. At the time of the Norman Conquest and after the death of King Harold, Edgar was the only legitimate Anglo Saxon heir to survive. After briefly resisting William the Conqueror, Edgar fled to Scotland, taking members of his family with him, including his sister Margaret who ultimately became the second wife of King Malcolm III. It was Margaret who first took a shine to William the Seemly Sinclair and she made him her cupbearer. It was from Margaret's husband, King Malcolm, that the Sinclairs received Roslin, their first lands in Scotland.

The Sinclairs prospered under successive Scottish kings. They also allied themselves to the Scandinavian Royal Families and ultimately came to control the Islands of Orkney, which had been subject to Nordic control and influence for centuries. In short the Sinclairs soon became one of the most powerful arms of the Scottish ruling elite.

At least part of the greatness of the Sinclairs stemmed from an uncanny ability to 'back the right horse' at times of political instability and what set them apart was their early mixed heritage – partly Norman French, and ultimately Scottish with strong Nordic connections.

The real upturn in the fortunes of the family came in 1379 when Henry Sinclair was awarded the title 'Earl of Orkney'. Orkney is a large island immediately to the north of the Scottish mainland. Its strategic importance in medieval times cannot be overstated, since anyone who controlled Orkney could also influence events in the north of Scotland itself. For centuries the island had been claimed by the kings of Norway. In 1379 the monarch of Norway was King Hakon and he found himself with a problem. The old line of Norwegian Earls or Jarls had died out and because of dynastic marriages the only logical candidate for the position was not Norwegian at all, it was Henry Sinclair – a Scotsman.

Henry Sinclair had inherited the family titles at a very early age. He was born around 1345 and his father had died when he was only thirteen years of age. At that time he became Baron of Roslin, Lord Chief Justice of Scotland and Admiral of the Seas. When he also became Earl of Orkney he immediately increased his family fortunes and also sowed the seeds of potential problems with the Scottish Crown.

The Henry Sinclair who became the first Earl of Orkney has gone down in history as 'Henry the Navigator'. Legend asserts that Henry was a great sailor and that he enlisted the support of a Venetian family by the name of Zeno, to embark on an epic voyage to America in or around the year 1380, a full century before the much more historically accepted voyage of Christopher Columbus. Many modern historians pour scorn on this suggestion, but as we shall see there is evidence within Rosslyn Chapel that may give it some credence.

When Henry Sinclair became Earl of Orkney and Shetland, to which the title also applied, the islands had been without an Earl for some years. As a result both places had become lawless and overrun with outlaws. King Hakon was hopeful that the appointment of a new Earl would mean the rule of law being re-established in both islands. Well aware of this fact the young Sinclair had a great castle built at Kirkwall. This would become the Sinclair headquarters and from here the islands were eventually subdued and brought to a peaceful and prosperous state.

Control of Orkney in particular would become crucial to Scotland, a country that by this time maintained an independent status, freed from control by its southern neighbour, England. But in Henry Sinclair's time ultimate control of Orkney, an island of immense strategic importance, lay far away in an unpredictable Scandinavia. Henry Sinclair was Earl of

Orkney but he did not own the place. On the contrary he governed it for the Norwegian Crown. This put Earl Henry between a rock and hard place, trying to serve the needs of the Scottish throne on the one hand and a Scandinavian king on the other.

Henry Sinclair steered a careful path – always seeking to show his loyalty to both kings, and when he died his title of Earl of Orkney passed to his son, another Henry. Ultimately, in 1422, the title came to William Sinclair, third Earl of Orkney and the builder of Rosslyn Chapel.

William Sinclair

William Sinclair was born in 1410. He seems to have received a good education and everything about his life shows him to have been a capable administrator, a shrewd operator but also a man of deeply philanthropic leanings. Although he was sometimes at odds with the Scottish crown in a legal sense, he never rebelled and always managed to steer a sensible and equitable course through the minefield of political allegiances that existed.

Throughout most of his life discussions continued between Scotland and Norway, with the specific aim on the part of the Scots crown of acquiring sovereignty over Orkney and Shetland. William would have been only too aware that if such a state of affairs came about he would lose one of his chief sources of revenue and so for years he spent much of his income privately buying land on Orkney that lay outside his Earldom and therefore royal control. The result was that when he lost the Earldom he continued to be a major landowner in Orkney and so his fortune did not significantly diminish. In fact he was so shrewd that when the Earldom ceased in 1470 he lost nothing but the title. He also retained his status because some twenty years earlier he had been given the title 'Earl of Caithness'.

Another proof of William Sinclair's shrewd nature is his handling of the situation regarding some of his southern estates, which lay in Nithsdale. William had acquired these lands when he had married his first wife, who was formerly Elizabeth Douglas. The Scottish king at the time wanted the land himself for reasons of national security. After some negotiation with James II William agreed to seed the lands to the crown, but only in exchange for equally productive land in Caithness, together with a significant cash settlement. This transaction took place immediately before

Rosslyn Castle, home of Earl William Sinclair. Photograph taken from Rosslyn Glen

the commencement of Rosslyn Chapel. The conclusion must be that in the mid-1450's William had cash to spare, since this was also a period during which his extensive holdings were paying a high yearly income.

Barbara E. Crawford, a historian whose knowledge of the Sinclairs is second-to-none, points out in *William Sinclair – Earl of Orkney and His Family, A Study in the Politics of Survival*, that there may have been a significant rift between William Sinclair and King James II, which she puts down to rancour regarding the question of Orkney, an issue that would not be settled until 1470. This rift, she suggests, occurred in 1456. The reason she arrives at this conclusion is because in the preceding years William Sinclair had been high in the King's favour, so much so that he enjoyed the rank of Chancellor of Scotland, whereas after 1456 he disappears from the Scottish Court altogether for a number of years. We understand why Crawford might come to this conclusion but there is no evidence that William was absent from Court because he was out of favour. As recently as 1455 he had gained the ancient Earldom of Caithness for himself and his heirs and there is every reason to believe that in 1456 he remained high in the King's estimation and trust. So what was happening in 1456 that demanded so much of William Sinclair's time that he withdrew from the Royal Court? There is only one tangible answer that meshes with a host of other events taking place at the same time – he was fully occupied in building Rosslyn Chapel!

Rather than frowning on William Sinclair, James II did him a singular favour in June 1456, for it is at this time that the King put his signature to a charter that made Roslin an official borough, complete with a fair, a weekly market day and a town cross. The document tells us that henceforth the market day will be on a Saturday and that the yearly fair will take place on the feast of St Simon and St Jude, which is celebrated on 28 October. This prestigious charter was granted by King James II on 13 June 1456 – supposedly at the very time William Sinclair had fallen from favour.

There is nothing strange about a high-ranking noble such as Earl William Sinclair choosing to build a church such as Rosslyn Chapel on his land. It was such a common practice that almost every parish church across Britain can be traced to one aristocratic family or another. Life throughout the medieval period was, even for many elevated members of society, brutish and short. Violence prevailed and in order to defend one's property and even one's life, it was often necessary to resort to aggression.

High-ranking noblemen were probably more violent than most and their actions, except in the case of Crusading, were invariably directed at other Christians. They knew very well that according to the laws of the Church to kill even one fellow-Christian would mean spending eternity in Hell. The only way to avoid this was to somehow curry favour with the Creator, in the hope that their sins would be absolved. Building a church would probably have seemed to be a good start. They were, by the standards of the times, attempting to buy their way into paradise.

After the Norman Conquest church building in England soared in popularity as new landowners sought to gain influence with the Almighty. The richer the aristocrat, the more ruthless he had probably been during his life. But greater wealth would mean he would also be able to build a grander church, and in the logic of the period size really did matter.

Collegiate churches

What does set Rosslyn Chapel apart is the type of church it was intended to be. Rosslyn, like forty other such institutions in Scotland and many in England is a 'collegiate church' and this makes it different in many ways from the normal parish church.

The word collegiate comes from the Latin 'collegium', which related to a community, corporation or a simple gathering together of individuals with a common interest. In the early days of guilds, for example those of stonemasons or goldsmiths, such institutions were often referred to as 'colleges'. The modern use of the word college derives from these collegiate churches, many of which supported almshouses, charities or places of education. The earliest collegiate churches go right back to the days of Charlemagne. According to strict ecclesiastical law, collegiate churches could only be planned and built with the express permission of the Pope and they stood aside from the usual regulations of parishes, which all fell under the jurisdiction of a Bishop.

Collegiate churches developed in a number of different ways but they were all responsive to a group of people – in reality a committee – who came together to supervise both the practical and the spiritual arrangements necessary to support their own respective institutions. Some of the collegiate churches in England became large and powerful institutions. The

word 'Minster' when applied to a particular church in England invariably
denotes that this building was once a collegiate church, for example York
Minster, Beverly Minster and Southwell Minster. Although some of these
eventually gained the status of cathedrals, they were all originally self
sufficient, with land and property to provide running capital, and they had
their own priest and laypersons who formed the college. In other cases the
necessary college was funded by a founding family.

Many of the collegiate churches in Scotland were built for the almost
exclusive use of particular powerful families and their retainers. Rosslyn
Chapel was typical of many Scottish collegiate churches in this regard.
There is also a suggestion that the proliferation of the collegiate churches in
the 15th century, particularly in Scotland, was a reaction to the corruption
within the monastic system at this time.

The first of the Scottish collegiate churches was that of St Andrews
in Fife, which was established in 1248. This was followed by Abernethy
in Perth, which was founded in 1328, having been built on the site of a
former Culdean and then Augustinian establishment, as was the case with
many Scottish Roman Catholic chapels. Other collegiate churches quickly
followed, with Rosslyn Chapel, more rightly the Collegiate Church of St
Matthew, being founded in 1446. There is no direct evidence of a place of
worship on this site prior to the 15th century.

Many fine collegiate churches survive in Scotland but none have the
richness of carving or the mystique that has become attached to Rosslyn
Chapel. This building stands alone, not only in Scotland but throughout
the whole of the British Isles and it is a treasure in every sense of the
word. In its time it may well have been seen as the Scottish university of
collegiate churches.

It would appear at first sight that what was eventually designed to stand
at Rosslyn was destined to be much more extensive than the chapel that
exists now. In the 1960s American naval engineers from the nearby Faslane
Naval Base undertook a solar scan of the ground surrounding Rosslyn
Chapel. This seemed to indicate the presence of foundations outside and
to the west of the present Chapel. It demonstrated that if the Chapel had
been completed it would have eventually formed the shape of an engrailed
cross, which is the symbol of the Sinclair family. The finished Chapel
would have included north and south transepts and a choir. Nevertheless

authors such as Knight and Lomas[3] suggest that everything apart from the chapel we see today, together with its Victorian additions in the west, which were built by the 4th Earl of Rosslyn in 1880-81, is nothing but a deliberate deception on the part of William Sinclair. In others words, despite the jutting pieces of masonry at the west end that look as though they should be attached to something else and regardless of the extensive foundations, Rosslyn Chapel is as William Sinclair intended it to be. They even offer expert architectural evidence that this is the case.

Knight and Lomas claim Rosslyn Chapel to be a deliberately created copy of the long-vanished temple of Solomon, or more probably a later temple on the same site, which once stood in far-off Jerusalem. Whether this is the case or not, William Sinclair could have had reasons of his own for wanting both Church authorities and visitors to 'believe' that Rosslyn Chapel would eventually form only the Lady Chapel of a much larger building, though he may have had no real intention of finishing the structure. If this was the case he was wise in obtaining permission to build, not a normal parish church but one with a collegiate foundation. Once permission had been granted by the Vatican he was more or less free to proceed in any way he wished.

William Sinclair's involvement

Great Barons such as Earl William Sinclair were busy people, often travelling extensively, invariably engaged in disputes of one sort or another and also committed to the support he offered to both the crowns, Scotland and Norway, which he was obliged to serve. Rosslyn Castle, close to the chapel, was certainly William Sinclair's most important stronghold, if only because it was so close to Edinburgh, the Scottish capital city and place of government, but it was far from being his only responsibility. Far to the north lay Orkney and Shetland, where William Sinclair must have spent a significant proportion of his time, and he had land-holdings in other parts of Scotland too. The 15th century was a time during which great nobles, like monarchs, regularly progressed between their manorial lands, partly to spread the expense of feeding a large retinue but also to 'fly the flag' and

---

3 *The Hiram Key* Christopher Knight and Robert Lomas, Element, London, 1997

to dispense law. When Earl William travelled he did so with a retinue of over 100 armed men. He could well afford to do so because there is much evidence to suggest that he was indeed wealthier than the King. At the time Rosslyn Chapel was commenced in 1456 he was Earl of Orkney, Earl of Caithness and Baron of Roslin. Indeed, as we have seen, he had just relinquished the title of Lord High Chancellor of Scotland, all of which probably made him the most powerful man in the Scotland of his day.

For these reasons it is impossible to envisage that William Sinclair was ever present during the building of Rosslyn Chapel for extended periods. Neither is it likely that he would have been qualified to make many of the decisions that were necessary for its construction. By this period architecture was a complex business and was the prerogative of those who had spent years familiarising themselves with the laws of mathematics and geometry. William may have been quite emphatic in his ideas for what Rosslyn Chapel should be, but his involvement could surely have been only supervisory, though it has to be born in mind that for several years after 1456 he was missing from the Scottish court. It is quite conceivable that much of this period was spent at Rosslyn, but on the other hand it remains a fact that Earl William had such extensive lands elsewhere that he must surely have been on the move for much of each year.

Despite giving what time and attention he could to the project, what William Sinclair would have needed most for the planning and completion of Rosslyn Chapel was someone with sufficient education and learning to first of all plan the projected building and then to be on site more often than the great lord himself could manage.

Such a character was available to Earl William, what is more he was an individual we know to have been under the earl's patronage at the time. His name was Sir Gilbert Haye and because of his background we thought it useful to take as close a look as possible at his life and the part he may have played in the conception and building of Rosslyn Chapel. What we discovered was a picture of a man who, though more or less forgotten today, was almost as well travelled as the famed Marco Polo, was well versed in many languages (at least sixteen!), and an expert in Latin, Greek, French, Hebrew and possibly Arabic. He had access to some of the most important books and manuscripts of his period and was familiar with Greek philosophers and ancient cultures generally. In short, he was a 15th century polymath!

4

Sir Gilbert Haye

Ancestry

GILBERT HAYE WAS born of a very important Anglo-Norman family that was descended from one William de la Haye, who came to Scotland from either England or Normandy as early as 1160 and who rose to the influential rank of 'Butler of Scotland'.

Though not specifically mentioned on the Battle Roll at Hastings, it is more or less certain that a knight with either the name or title of de la Haye was present with William the Conqueror at Hastings in 1066 when William, then Duke of Normandy, beat the English King Harold in battle and became the first of the Norman Kings of England. It is suggested that this knight did indeed have Scottish ancestry and that an aged relative who was chief of the Clan na Garadh called him to Scotland soon after 1066. The old chief died and so his de Haye relative became chief in his place. The na Garadh surname fell into disuse and that of Haye took its place.

William de la Haye was Butler of Scotland and Baron of Errol soon after 1160. This same William married a Celtic heiress from Pitmilly, near the estuary of the river Tay and soon became a trusted ally and adviser to the Scottish crown.

The Haye family connection with royalty did not diminish over the years. In 1255 and 1258 another Gilbert Haye, this one the third baron of Errol, held the title of co-Regent of Scotland. This took place during the minority of King Alexander III of Scotland who had come to the throne in 1249 at the tender age of eight years. The grandson of the third baron of Errol, yet another Sir Gilbert, was a staunch follower of the famed Robert the Bruce, who conferred upon him the hereditary and very important title of 'Constable of Scotland'. The family, through further royal patronage and judicial marriages, gained further influence and eventually owned large tracts of land in the Perthshire Highlands.

The French connection

It was into this illustrious family that the Gilbert Haye who is of most interest to us was born around 1403. We know little of his early life, though it can be assumed that he had a privileged upbringing because he is recorded as having attended St Andrews University, where his name is mentioned in 1418 and 1419. St Andrews is the oldest and most illustrious of the Scottish universities. It was founded in 1413, so Gilbert Haye would have been amongst its first students. There he gained degrees as both Bachelor and Master of Arts, and since he is soon mentioned as 'Sir' Gilbert Haye we can take it that he was also knighted around this time.

By 1432 Gilbert Haye is mentioned in documents as having been in France. This is not at all unlikely because during the reign of King Charles VII of France, which began in a tenuous way in 1422, a particularly close alliance arose between Scotland and France. One result of this was the formation of the 'Garde Ecossaise', an elite regiment of Scottish soldiers that eventually came to be the personal bodyguard of French monarchs. France was invariably at daggers drawn with England and from a Scottish point of view there was undoubtedly some mileage in the adage that 'my enemy's enemy is my friend'. Born of an illustrious and powerful family, Gilbert Haye, by this time in his late twenties, could easily have been a member

Gilbert Haye's French patron, King Charles VII

of the Garde Ecossaise, or he may have held an ambassadorial role at the French Court. Either way there is no doubting that this educated and clearly very bright man made a favourable impression in France because he stayed there for upwards of two decades.

Not only was Gilbert eventually made Chamberlain to the French King, for he tells us in the prologue to his book *Buke of the Law of Arrays* that he was 'Chaumerlayn umquhyle to the maist worthy King Charles of France,' but he may also have been at least partly responsible for Charles ever becoming king.

At the time Charles' father died in 1422, a treaty existed between France and England that had promised the French throne to the English Crown upon the death of Charles VI. This meant that when Charles VI died the throne of France should have come to King Henry VI of England. Popular sentiment in France repudiated the treaty with England, and help for the somewhat beleagured Charles came in the form of Joan of Arc. Born of a French peasant family the young Joan claimed to have been visited by God, who told her that Charles, at that time the dispossessed Dauphin, should proclaim himself to be King of France. Charles' banner was raised on 8 March 1429 and, after a famous victory over the English, Charles was crowned King Charles VII of France in Reims Cathedral on 17 July 1429. It is known that Sir Gilbert Haye was present, both when Joan first met Charles and later at his coronation. He occupied a place of honour and was most likely present as a representative of the Scottish Crown, which had its own reasons to deny the English King the French Crown. He was also personally knighted by the new French king.

It seems unlikely that Gilbert actually took part in the battles to free France from English domination – mainly because he was bookish by nature and there is no record of him ever being a soldier. A further indication of his personal leanings is the fact that Charles VII put Gilbert in sole charge of his personal library, which at the time was the toast of Europe and contained works from the four corners of the known world.

This would have given Gilbert access to the sum total of acquired human knowledge at the time. In addition, and during the time he was based in France, Gilbert undertook a series of journeys. He travelled to Italy, the Holy Land, parts of Africa and across much of Asia. In addition he also ventured as far as the almost legendary Cathay, which was the European name for China from the 14th century on. A list of his journeys, written in his own hand in the footnotes of one of his manuscripts, 'The Scotticum', bears testimony to his travels. The first European to visit distant Cathay and to catalogue his travels had been Maro Polo, who lived between 1254 and 1324. However, even by the 15th century little was known about the Far East and very few people travelled such a distance.

Throughout the period of his French residence Sir Gilbert Haye acquired more knowledge, copied books to which he had unique access and made himself one of the most educated individuals of his day. His importance to the French king cannot be underestimated, which makes it all the more mysterious that in 1456, by which time Gilbert was around 53 years of age, he is found once more in Scotland, where he supposedly took up the role of a simple teacher to the children of the Sinclair family at Rosslyn Castle. The actual year of his return is not known for certain and the date of 1456 is merely the first time he is mentioned in documents as having been once more resident in Scotland.

Frustratingly, there is no documented reason for Gilbert's sudden change of direction in life. Without doubt he was supremely fitted to become one of the most eminent Professors of his time, either in France or Scotland. He was not only an accomplished linguist, he was a bibliophile, historian, geographer and an accomplished statesman. It is possible that by his early to middle fifties, which was quite an advanced age during this period, Gilbert simply opted for a simpler life, and that he may have yearned for the land of his birth. The Sinclairs were rich patrons and Gilbert's duties as tutor to the Sinclair children would not have been onerous. But it is far more likely that Gilbert had come home for a very particular reason. It is our contention that Sir Gilbert Haye returned to Scotland in the pivotal year of 1456 specifically to take part in the building of Rosslyn Chapel, and indeed we have incontrovertible evidence of his involvement.

Connection of Gilbert Haye with Rosslyn

According to most accounts, permission to build the Collegiate Church of St Matthew at Rosslyn was granted in 1446, though as we shall see building almost certainly commenced at a later date. We know for certain that Gilbert Haye was present at Rosslyn by 1456 and he could have been there significantly earlier than this. But what leads us to the belief that Sir

Gilbert Haye not only contributed to but was probably instrumental in the planning and building of Rosslyn Chapel? It is the ultimate realisation that almost every facet of Gilbert's carefully acquired knowledge, his familiarity with religion and philosophy, his knowledge of far-away places and ancient legends have been carefully built into the tapestry in stone that Rosslyn Chapel represents.

Gilbert Haye had a wide-ranging mind and was fascinated by all manner of subjects. However, the surviving documents he has left to posterity point in specific directions. In particular we have surviving pieces of the only book we know for sure Gilbert wrote himself. This was *The Book of Alexander the Conqueror*, portions of which are still to be seen in Taymouth Castle. There also exist three volumes (bound together) that Gilbert translated from their original languages. These are:

The Buke of the Law of Armss or the Buke of Bataillis, a translation of a book by Honore Bonet that was originally entitled *Arbre des Batailles;* '*The Buke of the Order of Iinichthood',* taken from the '*Livre de l'ordre de chevalerie',*
and *The Buke of tile Governaunce of Princes,* culled from a French version of the pseudo-Aristotelian work originally titled '*Secrela Secrelorum'.*

By the time of Gilbert Haye, Alexander the Great, his life and conquests, had become a fabulous collection of mostly mythical stories, of which his

Detail from the carving of the Seven Deadly Sins in Rosslyn Chapel. There is a mistake in this carving echoing one of Gilbert Haye's own manuscripts

journey to Earthly Paradise was just one example. The point of this story seems to have been to indicate that no matter how powerful and successful a man's life might be, he was as subject to the laws of nature, ageing and death as any mortal. Whilst it might be suggested that there are strong Christian overtones to this story it also became a repository for Aristotlean philosophy at a time when the ruling hand of the established Church was at its most powerful and when philosophy, for a brief time, lay within the interest of three successive popes. Gilbert Haye shared the ideals and aspirations of these 15th cenutry popes, who were his contemporaries. As we shall see the stories of Alexander and his journey to Paradise are amply reflected in Rosslyn Chapel's carvings.

At the base of the Princes Pillar in Rosslyn Chapel there are eight fabulously carved dragons. Our research had demonstrated that these are undoubtedly Chinese in inspiration. There are also many carvings of a strongly Judaic or pre-Judaic style. Some of these relate to stories that are Babylonian in origin. These are all themes that fell within the remit of Sir Gilbert Haye.

The concluding piece of evidence is at the east end, where there is a detailed carving that represents the seven deadly sins. It can be observed that on this carving the sin of gluttony does not occupy its rightful place in the generally accepted list. We find the same mistake amongst Sir Gilbert Haye's writings, in which gluttony is identically displaced. There could hardly be more tangible or insistent evidence than this for his involvement in the chapel.

We are well aware that Sir William Sinclair, the man who was responsible for the planning and creation of Rosslyn Chapel, was an intelligent and astute man, but there is no indication that he was a scholar or that he had amassed the sort of knowledge necessary to lay down the many layers of religion and philosophy represented within the Chapel. However, Sir Gilbert Haye had all the necessary knowledge and experience and his surviving works and translations lock directly into the subject matter depicted within the Chapel. We conclude that there is ample evidence to prove beyond doubt that although it was Sir William Sinclair who sought permission for Rosslyn Chapel directly from the Pope and who supplied the manpower and money necessary for its construction, it was Sir Gilbert Haye who was responsible for its execution and who was the ultimate author of these 'volumes in stone'.

5

What's in a name?

LIKE MOST CHRISTIAN churches Rosslyn Chapel has a dedication. The habit of naming churches after a particular individual from the Christian story or any one of many hundreds of possible Catholic saints, goes back a very long way. Rosslyn Chapel is dedicated to one of the earliest characters from the story of Jesus. For their dedication William Sinclair and the other planners and builders of Rosslyn Chapel settled upon St Matthew.

St Matthew was one of the disciples of Jesus. He is first mentioned in the New Testament of the Bible in St Matthew, 9:9 when Jesus called upon him to become a follower.

'And as Jesus passed forth from thence, he saw a man, named Matthew, sitting at the receipt of custom: and he said unto him, Follow me. And he arose, and followed him.'

Matthew is mentioned another four times in the New Testament of the Bible: in Luke 6:15, Mark 3:18, Matthew 10:3 and in the Acts of the Apostles 1:13. He is listed as being one of the witnesses to Jesus' Resurrection and it is clear that he was one of the inner-circle of Jesus' disciples. But what really sets St Matthew apart is that he is generally recognised as having been the same St Matthew who wrote what was to become the first Gospel of the New Testament. His position as a Gospel writer has special significance because unlike the other Gospel writers, St Matthew had been present at the unfolding of the events he was later to chronicle for the early Christian Church.

Whether or not the Matthew of Jesus' ministry and the Matthew of the New Testament Gospel are the same person, it is clear that at the time the dedication of St Matthew was given to the brand new Rosslyn Chapel, everyone in Christendom made the association.

But what possible connection can there be between the life of St Matthew and the profusion of naturalistic carvings that adorn Rosslyn Chapel? In fact the answer is that there is a very real and tangible connection, at least in the minds of 15th century Christians. This is not because of anything the Bible says about St Matthew, but rather as a result of other writings, made by the early Church Fathers and accepted as 'gospel' by later Christians.

The Acts and Martyrdom of St Matthew

Many of the earliest writings of the Christian Church have been gathered together in a long work entitled *The Anti-Nicene Fathers*. This is a protracted collection of sayings, sermons, biographies of early Church characters and treatises on early Church doctrine. Amongst these, in Volume 8, is an exhaustive description of at least the later part of the life of St Matthew. Church authorities these days make it plain that this testimony is not historically reliable, as it is filled with fantastic happenings and impossible situations.

The Acts and Martyrdom of St Matthew, penned by an unknown writer but probably dating back as far as the 3rd century AD, gives a detailed account of St Matthew's last days, which were spent in a city referred to as 'Myrna'. This could have been in Northern Ethiopia or Turkey, though it is impossible to say with certainty.

There was already a church in Myrna by the time Matthew visited the place for what was the second time because the story makes it plain that it had a bishop, whose name was Plato. Matthew was alone outside Myrna, which strangely enough is often referred to in the tale as the place of the man-eaters. The story finds him in the midst of a forty-day fast, in what is essentially a desert. Whilst walking alone Matthew is visited by a child who he recognises as being one of the heavenly host but whom he does not immediately realise is a manifestation of Jesus himself. Matthew is troubled that he has nothing to offer this heavenly child and that there is not even any water at hand with which to wash his feet. But Jesus tells Matthew that:

> *'good discourse is better than a calf, that words of meekness better than any herb of the field, that a sweet saying is as good as the perfume of love. Cheerfulness of countenance is better than feeding and that a pleasant look is as the appearance of sweetness.'*

There follows a lengthy discourse in which Matthew assumes that the child may be one of the children who were supposedly killed by King Herod in his search for Jesus when he too was still an infant, of which, according to this particular story, there were three thousand.

The Jesus-child hands Matthew a staff. He tells him to take it to Myrna, to the gate of the church that Matthew and another apostle, Andrew, had founded there earlier. There he is to drive the staff into the ground. He tells Matthew:

> *'as soon as thou hast planted it, it shall be a tree, great and lofty and with many branches, and its branches shall extend to thirty cubits, and of each single branch the fruit shall be different both to the sight and the eating, and from the top of the tree shall flow down much honey; and from its root there shall come forth a great fountain, giving drink to this country round about, and in it creatures that swim and creep; and in it the man-eaters shall wash themselves, and eat of the fruit of the trees of the vine and of the honey.'*

Matthew gathers together the believers and non-believers of Myrna and tells them:

> *'I shall plant this rod in this place, and it shall be a sign to your generations, and it shall become a tree, great and lofty and flourishing, and its fruit beautiful to the view and good to the sight; and the fragrance*

*of perfumes shall come forth from it, and there shall be a vine twining
round it, full of clusters; and from the top of it honey coming down, and
every flying creature shall find covert in its branches; and a fountain of
water shall come forth from the root of it, having swimming and creeping
things, giving drink to all the country round about.'*

Matthew's staff

So saying Matthew plants the staff in the ground and, as prophesied, it
quickly grows into a tall and beautiful tree. The countryside around the
tree becomes green and verdant and creatures of all kinds appear, together
with fountains of water and honey falling from the top of the great tree.

The remainder of the story details Matthew's struggle with the King of
Myrna, whose name is Fulvanus. The king fears Matthew and also hates
him. He seeks by every means possible to kill the apostle but is thwarted
at every turn until Matthew himself concedes that it is time for him to
pass away and journey to Paradise. Fulvanus has Matthew nailed down
and places all manner of combustible material on him in order to burn
his body to ashes but Matthew is untouched by the flames. The apostle
causes the flames to pursue the king and to destroy his army, and he also
summons up a fearful dragon that pursues the king into his palace. When
Fulvanus begs for mercy the flames are extinguished and the dragon
disappears. At around the sixth hour Matthew voluntarily passes away and
his spirit is seen to be taken up into heaven.

Wishing to rid himself of the body of the apostle King Fulvanus has
Matthew sealed with lead into an iron coffin, which he instructs should be
loaded on a boat, rowed out to sea and then thrown in the water. Early the
next day, as everyone including the king stands and watches in disbelief,
the iron coffin is born back to shore by a heavenly host. King Fulvanus
now repents and surrenders himself to Plato, who baptises him. When the
bishop, Plato, dies, three years later, the king surrenders his crown and,
taking the name of Matthew, becomes bishop in his place.

Fanciful though this tale may seem in the 21st century, there is little
doubt that the majority of believers in the 15th century would have
accepted it as being a true account of events surrounding the last days
and the death of St Matthew. The story would have been well known,

especially to ecclesiastics, and Earl William could quite convincingly have suggested that the whole Chapel was merely a representation in stone of the events detailed in the story of St Matthew.

We have already mentioned the pillar known variously as the Princes Pillar or the Apprentice pillar. This is one of three significant pillars at the eastern end of the chapel and is the one that stands to the right, not far from the entrance to the sacristy and crypt. It is the most ornate of all the chapel's pillars and it is the piece of sculpture that attracts the most attention these days.

There are pictures of the pillar in the colour section. The pillar itself is of a fluted design, but around it are spirals of rich vegetation. At its base there are imaginatively carved dragons and the pillar rises to meet and support two of the ornate arches that adorn this part of the chapel.

The builders of Rosslyn Chapel would have had no difficulty whatsoever persuading any Church dignitary that this pillar, which is more rightfully known as 'the Prince's Pillar' is a representation of the tree that grew from the staff given to St Matthew by the Jesus child, complete with the vines that circled its broad trunk. It is from this pillar that all the carved vegetation in the chapel ultimately springs, and the botanical carvings do not touch ground level anywhere else in the building except at the base of the Prince's Pillar.

The tale of St Matthew tells us that the tree will engender many sorts of plants and fruits, and as we have seen there are many different species represented throughout the chapel. The story also relates that honey will fall from the top of the tree and as visitors these days who climb the gantry surrounding the chapel can see for themselves, one of the pinnacles at the east end has been deliberately created as a hive for wild bees, which still fly around the roof in the summer months.

As proof of the importance of St Matthew and the story outlined above, there exists a strange little picture of Rosslyn Castle, as it must have appeared prior to its partial destruction in the English Civil War of the 17th century. This drawing, created by an unknown hand, shows the eastern façade of the Castle. In the whole of this picture only one human form is present. This is the incongruous depiction of a man wearing robes. He is holding a staff and reaching out towards a majestic tree. So out of place is this character in what is clearly meant to picture Rosslyn Castle that there is little doubt he was intended to represent St Matthew, together with his magical staff and the tree that it became. We reproduce this picture below.

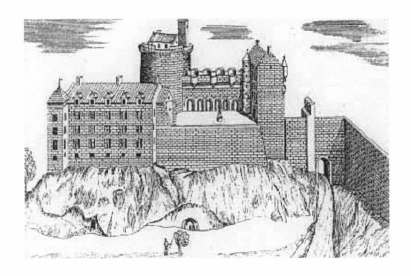

Is this then the very simple answer to the conundrum of Rosslyn Chapel? Are we to see in its breathtaking representations in stone nothing more or less than a depiction of a story relating to the Saint who gave his name to the chapel when it was first conceived in the minds of its creators, Earl William Sinclair and Sir Gilbert Haye? Hardly. There are many depictions in stone within the chapel that clearly have nothing whatsoever to do with the story of St Matthew and his magical staff. In any case, the story cannot explain why some of the plant species depicted represent botanical specimens that were unknown in 15th century Scotland. Neither does the story of St Matthew explain the only inscription in words within the stonework:

'Wine is strong, a king is stronger, women are stronger still but the truth conquers all.'

The story of St Matthew does not explain the significance of the Crypt and Sacristy, and it quite singularly fails to throw light on the proliferation of Green Men in the chapel, the legions of angels or any one of a hundred different puzzles. But it could be the reason why Earl William was not dragged before the Inquisition in chains for creating what could be seen as a very unchristian church building.

The dangers of heresy

The 15th century was a pivotal time for the Catholic Church. The institution was on the verge of collapsing under its own internal corruption and the greed of its rulers. A series of popes had occupied the throne of St Peter whose whole reason for gaining the papacy had been to line their own pockets and glorify their own names and that of their families. As early as 1342 Pope Clement VI, birth name Pierre Roger, having run short of money to fulfil his grandiose schemes for glorifying himself and his dynasty, instigated a process that would nearly prove to be the death-knell of the Catholic Church. He began the 'selling of indulgences'.

Under an official Papal bull, known as 'Unigentius', priests could henceforth grant Catholics remission from sins on the payment of a specific amount of money. The reasoning behind this practice was ostensibly to allow people the ability to gain the same spiritual favours as they would by embarking on a pilgrimage. The Church recognised that such protracted journeys would not be possible for some individuals, for a host of reasons. They suggested that a monetary sacrifice could be considered equal to the labours of a pilgrimage.

Of course the Church at every level, from the Parish Priest to the Pope himself, gained financially from the wholesale selling of indulgences, which nevertheless proved extremely popular and served to swell the coffers of the Vatican for centuries.

But not everyone was taken in, and especially not certain members of the lower clergy who were genuinely fired by religious zeal rather than personal greed. It was the selling of indulgences, together with the cult of religious relics, which ultimately led to a major split within the Catholic Church. This would not actually take place until the 16th century but there were opponents to the decadent lives led by Popes, Cardinals and Bishops long before. Already, in the 15th century, the Church was under attack and it fought back ferociously.

Nowhere was the Catholic Church more vicious than with those that it maintained were 'perverting' the Christian message. Anyone who said or did the wrong thing was likely to find him or herself summoned to Rome, where they could be subjected to the much-feared inquisition, a body that had the power of life and death over anyone. Radicals and freethinkers were regularly burned at the stake – and this could be anyone whose ideas appeared to differ in any way from orthodox Catholic doctrine.

Even far off Scotland was not beyond the long arm of Papal law and we can be certain that the sheer magnificence of Rosslyn Chapel, once it was finished, would have attracted the attention of local Church dignitaries such as bishops and cardinals, who would have taken a significant interest in the many carvings that might not, at first sight, appear to be wholly Christian in inspiration.

We can imagine a hypothetical visit, made by an emissary of the Pope to view the wonders of Rosslyn Chapel at first hand. Earl William would first take the red-coated cardinal to the Prince's Pillar. 'Of course,' he would say, 'you are quite familiar with the story of St Matthew and his visit to the City of Myrna; of how he was given the staff by the child-Jesus and planted it at the gate of the church?' The cardinal would nod wisely. 'Well here it is', Earl William would have said, 'captured for all time in stone, complete with the vine entwined around its trunk.' He may have turned and swept an arm around the building. 'As you know, in this most wonderful story there is a description of all the plants that grew from that one tree, of the fabulous animals that appeared, and here, at the base of the pillar, you can see the dragons sent by the blessed St Matthew to pursue the errant King into his palace.'

The cardinal, doubtless a man of some culture and breeding, would have marvelled at the artistry of the many hundreds of carvings that surrounded him, deep cut and new, vibrant with colour and creating exactly the sort of paradise that is described in the St Matthew story. He could not fail to be impressed and would surely have reported back to his own masters that Earl William was a true son of the Church and that his creation was a masterpiece of veneration to the memory of the blessed St Matthew and the glory of God.

But what was it about St Matthew and his adoption as the patron of Rosslyn Chapel that caused us to uncover something even more fantastic than anything dreamed up by Dan Brown in his blockbuster novel *The Da Vinci Code*?

6

The St John connection

21 September

EVERY CHRISTIAN APOSTLE and saint has a day on which his or her feast is celebrated. Such days in the Church year often relate to the date of their death, though of course many of them died so long ago that the chosen date may turn out to be one of convenience rather than accuracy. The English poet William Wordsworth was the first man to suggest that the geographical orientation of any British church was tied directly to the feast day of its patron saint, and subsequent research has shown this to be true in a large majority of cases.

Wherever possible Christian churches in the West have always been built in such a way that their altars faced east – towards Jerusalem. Judging which way true east might be is not as easy as it sounds, at least not without a compass. However, it is in the east that the sun, moon, planets and stars can be seen to rise on any day or night, before they take their journeys across the sky to set in the west. The only problem is that the 'part' of the eastern horizon where they rise is not 'true' east at all, except on two days each year.

Such is the nature of the Earth's orbit around the sun that it appears, from the point of view of earthbound observers, that the sun, planets and

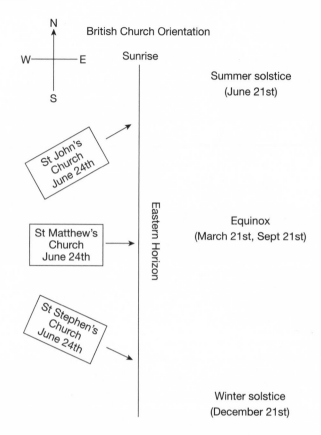

Churches were usually built so that their eastern ends faced towards the place of sunrise on the day of the feast of their patron saint. This meant that east was a 'relative' term and particularly in northern latitudes this could range from north east to south east.

stars rise at different points of the eastern horizon throughout any given year. If we take the sun as our reference and assume a northern hemisphere setting, the sun rises well south of east in midwinter, known as the winter solstice. Conversely it rises well north of east at midsummer, which is known as the summer solstice. Midway between these two points, in spring and autumn, there are those special days, called the spring and autumn equinox, when the sun rises due east and sets due west.

When a medieval church was being planned, its architects would spend some time observing the eastern horizon at dawn. In particular they would look for the position of the rising sun above the eastern horizon on the feast day of the saint whose dedication would be carried by the church.

As an example, if the Church was going to be dedicated to St Edmund, the English martyr, the day in question would be 21 November. A sighting would be taken for the position of the rising sun on this day, and this position would represent east as far as that church was concerned. In other words the east end of the finished building would point to this particular part of the horizon.

This is why so many British churches have slightly varying compass orientations – because different saints were celebrated on differing days, at which time the sun would occupy a unique position on the eastern horizon at dawn.

In Western Christianity St Matthew's Day is celebrated on 21 September, which is a very special day in the calendar because it is also the day on which the Autumn Equinox occurs – a day on which the sun rises due east. As a result we would expect Rosslyn Chapel to have an east end that faces due east, and indeed it does.

This particular time of the year has always been held by humanity as being special and sacred. In temperate climates in the northern hemisphere 21 September has invariably been seen as the date on which harvest commenced. To farming communities the harvest was of the utmost importance because, if anything went dramatically wrong leading up to it, like unseasonable and inclement weather, the result during the coming winter could be famine.

It was for this reason that both before and after the advent of Christianity this period of September was always a time of both celebration and sacrifice – celebration for the bounty of the harvest and sacrifices that were necessary to appease the gods and to ensure their co-operation henceforth. It was also recognised in many religions that, with the harvest, nature herself was making a supreme sacrifice. As we pointed out in Chapter 2, in the majority of ancient religions the supreme deity was the Goddess, who was synonymous with the Earth. Her offspring was all that grows in the earth, including the cereals that fed humanity.

We soon began to suspect that the dedication of St Matthew had been chosen very deliberately by Earl William Sinclair when he had decided to create his own collegiate church at Rosslyn. The association between St Matthew's Day, the Autumn Equinox and the significance this had to the proliferation of animistic and naturalistic carvings within Rosslyn Chapel seemed far from being coincidences. We had also noted the fact that the proliferation of Green Men within the chapel, together with the strong botanical theme, smacked at a memory of the 'Corn God' and his association with ancient religion and the divine mysteries – all of which were a legacy of Scotland's first animistic monks, the Culdeans.

The Gospel of Matthew in Hebrew

It seemed prudent to learn more, not only about Matthew himself but about the circumstances under which his Gospel and other writings concerning him had been produced. The Gospels themselves told us very little. We know that Matthew was sometimes called 'Levi', that his father had been called Alpheus and that Matthew himself was a tax collector. This meant he had to be educated, probably more so that most of the other disciples of Jesus who were, after all, simple fishermen. According to the Gospels Matthew was present on the morning Jesus was discovered to have risen from his tomb, and he was also one of the disciples who saw Jesus ascend into heaven.

Beyond this we have nothing from Bible sources and we cannot even be certain that the Matthew who wrote the Gospel that carries his name was the same Matthew who is mentioned as being one of the original disciples. The early Church Fathers were emphatic that this was the case and they were also very definite about one other fact – that St Matthew's Gospel had originally been written in either Aramaic or Hebrew, because these were the languages that would have been spoken in the area of Jesus' ministry.

If Matthew's account was a first-hand reporting of the events before and after the life of Jesus, and if it was intended for a local audience, there would be little point in the Gospel being written first of all in Greek.

The reason that many modern scholars have cast doubt on the Hebrew or Aramaic Gospel of St Matthew is primarily because of the controversy regarding the order in which the four Gospels of the New Testament of the Bible were written. Whilst very early sources are adamant that they were written in the order in which they appear in the New Testament: Matthew, Mark, Luke and John, more recent scholars say this cannot be the case.

The Gospels of St Matthew, St Mark and St Luke are known as 'the synoptic gospels'. These Gospels carry the name because of the work of

Johan Jakob Griesbach, a German biblical critic who lived between 1745 and 1812. Griesbach noted the similarities between the first three Gospels and in order to better study them he wrote them down in a three column table that he named 'a synopsis'. The similarities between the three Gospels came to be known as the Synoptic Problem.

Matthew, Mark and Luke are often very similar to each other in the way the story of Jesus is told, but they are all quite different from the Gospel of St John. Backtracking, as it were, it seemed to be apparent to fairly modern investigators that the Gospel of St Mark must have been written down first, simply because both St Matthew and St Luke appeared to be copying phrases from Mark. However, they both also had themes that appeared to come from another work, which has disappeared. For the sake of the argument this source has always been referred to as 'Q'.

Obviously, if it was known that the Gospel of Mark had originally been transmitted in Greek and Matthew had used phrases from this, it stood to reason that it was unlikely that Matthew's account had originally been written in Hebrew or Aramaic. The 'Two Source' theory, as it was known, became so popular that any thought of a non-Greek Gospel of Matthew was dismissed out of hand. This was fine, but there was a problem that would not go away, because Hebrew examples of the Gospel of St Matthew had emerged from time to time during the previous two thousand years. This did not particularly upset the adherents of the Two Source theory. They simply asserted that the original Greek copy of Matthew's Gospel had, at some time in the past, been translated into Hebrew – probably for the sake of a converted Judaic audience. Just because Hebrew copies of the Gospel of St Matthew existed in Hebrew, this did not mean they had been written in Hebrew in the first instance.

This seemed to explain the situation satisfactorily, until a definitive copy of an entire version of St Matthew's Gospel in Hebrew was recognised. It had been copied by a 13th century Spanish/Jewish physician whose name was Shem-Tob ben-Issac ben-Shaprut Ibn Shaprut. There was no doubt at all about the fact that this copy of a Hebrew St Matthew appeared in the 13th century, even if the document from which Shem-Tob had undertaken his copy no longer exists. This particular Hebrew Gospel of St Matthew appears in a work by Shem-Tob that was entitled 'Even Bochan'.

Once this had been closely studied it became obvious that it could not be a Greek Matthew's Gospel that had been translated into Hebrew, simply because it contained passages that were essentially different from the Gospel of St Matthew as we know it today. An English translation of this document does exist. It was undertaken by George Howard, Emeritus Professor of the Department of Religion and Professor of Religion at the University of Georgia in the US.[4]

George Howard came to the conclusion that whatever source had been used by Shem-Tob, this was not a simple translation into Hebrew of an originally Greek work. He based his conclusions mainly on the linguistic structure of the document, which, as an expert in Hebrew, he suggested could never have been a translation from Greek. He also observed that there were significant differences between the Hebrew and the Greek Gospels of St Matthew, even to the extent that some of the linguistic puns within the Gospel that don't work well or at all in Greek, do so much better in Hebrew.

There are many passages in Shem-Tob's Hebrew Gospel of St Matthew that do not appear in the Greek version and substantial sections of the Greek Matthew's Gospel that are not included in the Shem-Tob Matthew's Gospel. Taking everything into account Howard is quite certain that the Shem-Tob version was written for a wholly Jewish audience. So perplexed was Shem Tob himself by some of the passages he copied, even from his standpoint as a Jewish rather than a Christian scholar, that he had left notes to express his surprise at how different they were from the orthodox Gospel.

Although there are significant similarities between the Greek and accepted St Matthew's Gospel and the Shem-Tob Hebrew version, there are three very noticeable ways in which they vary consistently. Firstly, the Hebrew Gospel of St Matthew does not commence until the baptising of Jesus by John the Baptist – in other words there is no Nativity. In addition, nowhere in the Hebrew St Matthew is Jesus ever referred to as being 'the Messiah'. Finally, in Shem-Tob's Hebrew Gospel of Matthew, John the Baptist plays a much more important role and, unlike the Greek version, he is not sidelined in favour of Jesus.

If Professor Howard is to be believed it is impossible to imagine that the Hebrew St Matthew's Gospel of Shem-Tob could ever have been

---

4 *The Gospel of Matthew According to a Primitive Hebrew Text*, George Howard, Mercer University Press, 1987

copied from its Greek counterpart, though highly likely that the situation was the other way around. This still does not explain the similarities between Matthew's Gospel and that of Mark but it seems to us that one could conjecture a hypothesis in which parts of Mark were copied from an earlier Matthew, and that the Gospel of St Mark was subsequently used for source material by the author of St Luke's Gospel.

Shem-Tob's is not the only Hebrew version of the Gospel of St Matthew that has survived. Another example, known as the 'DuTillet Version', was supposedly found by Bishop Jean DuTillet, whilst he was visiting Rome in the middle of the 1550s, and a third, known as the Munster Matthew, was located by Sebastian Munster, (1488-1552). Munster was originally a German Franciscan Monk, but after the Reformation in Germany he became a follower of Luther. However, the validity of these translations remains in doubt, because in each case the translator had an axe to grind, and knowingly made alterations in order to fit the Hebrew text to the Greek Gospel.

All of this brought us to lines of investigation we had not expected to undertake. From the start we intended to look at Rosslyn Chapel openly, relying wherever possible on extant historical sources, whilst avoiding legend and hearsay as much as possible. Despite this we had both been studying Rosslyn Chapel for a very long time and we were as familiar with the many stories associated with the building as anyone. Two of the most enigmatic groups of people that have been strongly associated with Rosslyn Chapel – in popular legend if not in provable historical fact – are the Knights Templar and Freemasons.

The Knights Templar was an order of fighting monks that originated in Champagne in the early 12th century. The Templars, or more properly 'The Poor Fellow Soldiers of Christ and the Temple of Solomon', went on to become the most powerful, rich and influential monastic order the West would ever know. Far from remaining a bunch of poor monks, they virtually built the economic foundation of what would become modern Europe.

The Templars had, and the Freemasons still maintain, a particular and very special reverence for John the Baptist. In the case of the Templars it has been repeatedly suggested that John the Baptist took precedence over Jesus in their estimation and religious practices.

John the Baptist is mentioned in the Greek versions of the Christian gospels and in tradition is supposed to have been the cousin of Jesus. John – a desert-living hermit who preached to multitudes by the River Jordan – is depicted in the gospels as being Jesus' herald and the one who ultimately baptised Jesus himself, before the start of his own mission.

The assertion that the Knights Templar had a particular fascination for St John the Baptist has come, over the years, from a number of often-strange sources. A good example of this is an extract from a book by the Theosophist Madam H P Blavatsky, a Russian of fairly elevated birth. She was born in 1831 and was destined to travel the world extensively. On the way she developed a penchant for the mystical and spiritual.

In her book *Isis Unveiled*[5] which was written in 1877, Blavatsky had this to say about the Knights Templar:

'The true version of the history of Jesus, and the early Christianity was imparted to Hugh de Payens, by the Grand-Pontiff of the Order of the Temple (of the Nazarene or Johannite sect), one named Theocletes, after which it was learned by some Knights in Palestine, from the higher and more intellectual members of the St. John sect, where were initiated into its mysteries. Freedom of intellectual thought and the restoration of one and universal religion was their secret object. Sworn to the vow of obedience, poverty, and chastity, they were at first the true Knights of John the Baptist, crying in the wilderness and living on wild honey and locusts. Such is the tradition and the true kabalistic version.'

Much more recently we find in the seminal work *The Holy Blood and the Holy Grail* by Baigent Leigh and Lincoln[6]:

'Certain writers have suggested that the Templars were 'infected' with the Johannite or Mandaean heresy – which denounced Jesus as a 'false prophet' and acknowledged John [the Baptist] as the true Messiah. In the course of their activities in the Middle East the Templars undoubtedly established contact with Johannite sects.'

From where had Madam Blavatsky and the authors of the Holy Blood and

---

5 *Isis Unveiled*, H P Blavatsky, Theosophical University Press, 1972
6 *The Holy Blood and the Holy Grail*, Baigent, Leigh, Lincoln, A Delacorte Press, 1982

the Holy Grail culled this extraordinary information? In fact it had come from the Catholic Church itself. In the 'Allocution of Polo Nono against the Freemasons', a 19th century Church Bull from the pontificate of Pope Pius IX we are told:

'The Johannites ascribed to Saint John the Baptist the foundation of their Secret Church, and the Grand Pontiffs of the Sect assumed the title of Christos,[7] *Anointed, or* Consecrated, *and claimed to have succeeded one another from Saint John by an uninterrupted succession of pontifical powers. He who, at the period of the of the foundation of the Order of the Temple, claimed these imaginary prerogatives, was named Theoclet; he knew Hughes de Payens,(* the first Grand Master of the Templars*) he installed him into the Mysteries and hopes of his pretended church, he seduced him by the notions of Sovereign Priesthood and Supreme royalty, and finally designated him as his successor.'*

Pope Pius IX (1846 – 1878)

Could there be any truth in this extraordinary claim? If nothing else these Papal words do suggest that the Catholic Church accepted, and probably always had accepted, that there was a definite connection between Templarism, which was destroyed at the start of the 14th century, and Freemasonry, which still proliferates in the world today. This is made plain because in 'Allocution of Polo Nono against the Freemasons', Pope Pius IX was railing not against the Templars, who after all no longer existed, but at what he considered to be their modern manifestation, Freemasons.

Freemasons from around the world flock into Rosslyn Chapel on any day of the week throughout the whole year. Some of these people willingly travel thousands of miles on what can only be seen as a pilgrimage. Whether or not there is any incontrovertible proof of the connection of Freemasonry to Rosslyn Chapel seems to be beside the point to most of

---

7 It is interesting to note that the original name of the Templars was 'The Poor Fellow-soldiers of Christ and the Temple of Solomon' but they were never called 'The Poor Fellow-soldiers of Jesus Christ and the Temple of Solomon.'

them. Neither is the affinity Freemasons feel for the Chapel something that has been promoted by fanciful 20th or 21st century writers, because Freemasons have venerated the Chapel for as long as the Craft has existed.

Freemasons tell their own tales about the Chapel, make their own explanations regarding many of its carvings and, in short, have no doubt that their own fraternal calling is inextricably linked to this one, special building. Many Freemasons today, probably the majority, also believe emphatically that there is a direct connection between their own Craft and those mysterious fighting monks, the Knights Templar.

As far as the possible heresy of the Knights Templar is concerned we fortunately have more to go on than the opinions of a 19th century pope. The Templars were renounced and declared heretic in 1307. Many Templars were arrested and put on trial. Evidence pointing to a strongly Johannite core at the heart of Templarism came to light during the trials of Templar knights that took place in the months after October 1307.

In particular the inquisitors were fascinated with a mysterious bearded head, which, it was said, was worshiped by the Templars. This head, referred to in the trials as 'Baphomet' was equated at the time with the preserved head of John the Baptist, which the Templars were said to have in their possession. Some senior Templars at their trials suggested that the head had specific powers to: 'make trees blossom and the land to produce'.

If the Templars did venerate John the Baptist they were not alone. Johannite sects from history most certainly did exist, in fact they still do. There is a small group of dissident believers living in the modern State of Iraq who call themselves Mandaeans. They may have originated in Persia but are thought to have been living in Palestine at the time Christianity

A 16th century representation of John the Baptist

came into being. The Mandaeans are often considered these days to be a Gnostic Christian sect, but they do not accept either Christianity or Islam.

The Mandaeans have a particular regard for John the Baptist and they call Jesus the 'false Messiah'. It is possible that their respect for John the Baptist stems in part from his habit of baptizing converts, a practice that is of the utmost importance to the Mandaeans themselves. But the Mandaeans are the legatees of another sect from Palestine that flourished at the beginning of the modern era. This was the sect of the 'Ebionites'.

The Ebionites

The Ebionites are known to have existed at the time of the very early Church. The word Ebionites comes from a root Aramaic word that means 'Poor Men'[8]

The doctrines of the Ebionites were explained by Irenaeus, who was born in Ephesus, Turkey. He eventually became Bishop of Lyon in France and died around 202. Irenaeus fought a lifelong battle against Christian "heretics" at a time when the "orthodox" Church, as it eventually developed, didn't really exist at all. Writing about the Ebionites, he claimed they did not believe in either the Virgin Birth of Jesus, or his rank of Messiah. They repudiated the teachings of St Paul and they relied on only one Gospel, this being the Hebrew version of the Gospel of St Matthew! They also revered John the Baptist as being a crucially important messenger, but believed he was no more the Son of God than was Jesus.

Another book the Ebionites revered was the 'Hypomnemata' against the canonical Gospel of St Matthew. This was written by Symmachus, a 2nd century Ebionite, who also translated versions of the Old Testament of the Bible. We would dearly love to see what Symmachus had to say about the now authorised version of St Matthew's Gospel but, alas, the document no longer exists.

At least a section of the Ebionites became, with the passing of time, a deeply Gnostic sect. They came to believe that matter is eternal and that it literally represents God's body. Thus, to them, matter was pre-existent

---

8 Contrast 'poor men' with 'poor fellow-soldiers', which is what the Templars were called.

and Creation merely represented a transformation of existing material. The instrument God uses for his purposes is wisdom, which in Greek is the word 'Sophia'.

Sophia is a word that has strong feminine overtones. It was the original word used by early Christians for the Holy Spirit. Meanwhile, 'Baphomet', the word that had surfaced during the trials of the Templars, was looked at carefully by the late Dr Hugh Schonfield. Schonfield was an academic who had worked extensively on the Dead Sea Scrolls. He applied the word Baphomet to an ancient Jewish cipher that had regularly been used in Old Testament times. This was known as the 'Atbash Cipher'. Using this cipher the word Baphomet became 'Sophia'.

According to the Ebionites this Sophia, or wisdom, is what created and continues to create the world and everything in it. They also talked about an intermediary between God and Man who they referred to as 'The Son of God', a character who may or may not be equated with Jesus. But even if it is Jesus, it is certainly not Jesus the man, but rather his possession of Sophia, brought down to him in the form of a dove when John baptised him in the waters of the River Jordan. Neither did the Gnostic Ebionites believe that Jesus could have been literally the 'Son of God', at least no more than any other mortal, simply because nothing could compare with God.

According to the Gnostic Ebionites nobody could be saved simply by believing in Jesus, or any other messenger for that matter. The only path to salvation was knowledge (Gnosis) and by believing in 'God the Teacher'. They did however accept baptism as a means of the remission of sins.

Like another Jewish sect with whom they were said to be associated, the Essenes, the Ebionites believed that a constant war between good and evil, or, more properly in their symbolism, between darkness and light, was being fought. According to the *New Catholic Encyclopaedia*[9], Ebionite beliefs encapsulate: '*Pantheism , Persian Dualism, Judaism, and Christianity fused together.*' There could scarcely be a better description of the themes we find in Rosslyn Chapel.

In their original form the Ebionites were a mostly Jewish sect. However, there were gentile members too and they are known to have professed a need for all believers to adhere to what were known as the 'Noahide Laws'.

---

9 *New Catholic Encyclopaedia*, Published by Gale, 1967

These were thought of as the laws given by God to the prophet Noah after the Flood, and long before the time of Moses. There were seven Noahide Laws, which were as follows:

1. The worship of false Gods is forbidden.
2. Murder is forbidden.
3. Theft and kidnapping is forbidden.
4. Sexual immorality is forbidden.
5. It is forbidden to bless God *(which really means blasphemy is forbidden.)*
6. It is forbidden to eat flesh torn from a living animal. *(In practice many of the Ebionites, like the Essene, seem to have been vegetarians.)*
7. It is not permitted to allow oppression or anarchy to rule. Set up a system of honest, effective courts, police and laws to uphold the last six laws.

The "original Christians"

In 2006 James D Tabor published a significant new book summarising the new thinking on John, Jesus and Paul. He is a noted biblical archaeologist, a respected scholar and a Professor in the Department of Religious Studies at the University of South Carolina at Charlotte, US.

Professor Tabor had been visiting and excavating in the Near East for decades and is an undoubted expert on bible history. What led him to write *The Jesus Dynasty*[10] was his gradual realisation that the story of Jesus as related by the Gospels of Matthew, Mark, Luke and John had been manipulated by forces that came into being after the events the Gospels purport to chronicle.

Tabor believes that the part played in the New Testament by John the Baptist had originally been much more important than the surviving gospels indicate, and he has spent decades carefully picking away at the evidence in order to try and establish the truth. He acknowledges the importance of the surviving Hebrew version of St Matthew's Gospel but also lays great store by the mysterious 'Q' Gospel, the lost work upon which Matthew and

---

10 *The Jesus Dynasty*, James D Tabor, Harper Element, 2006

Mark relied heavily when penning their own stories. By stripping out from the Gospels all information that was obviously from a third party source, Tabor was able to recreate 'Q', and when he did so he discovered that the story it was telling about Jesus and the events that unfolded during his era were radically different than the version offered by the accepted Gospels.

Tabor reaches the conclusion that during his lifetime Jesus never declared himself to be, or thought of himself as, the one and only Messiah. Rather he was the important, but temporary leader of a Davidic sect of Judaism that believed in the coming of God's Kingdom to Earth. Closely allied to the Essene, and their beliefs, Jesus had followed his relative John the Baptist as leader of this sect and was in turn followed by his brother James.

Professor Tabor suggests that the true legatees of John, Jesus and James were the Ebionites, the schismatic Christian sect that survived for centuries after orthodox Christianity developed. He also places great emphasis on the fact that the Ebionites repudiated St Paul, whom they accused of being the individual most responsible for the perversion of the original message of the new sect. Tabor's ultimate conclusion is that it was John the Baptist, not Jesus, who was the founder of this revolutionary form of Judaism and that during his lifetime Jesus regularly acknowledged the fact.

Many scholars believe that after the death of Jesus the Ebionites were followers of his brother James. In the New Testament of the Bible it is clear that James, usually referred to as James the Just, was often at odds with St Paul. St Paul, whose real name was Saul, although not one of the original disciples, went on to have a massive bearing on the way Christianity would develop. Whilst James remained in and around Jerusalem, where he was murdered, most likely about 62 AD, Paul travelled extensively. According to tradition St Paul was ultimately martyred in Rome, having insisted on being tried there because he was a Roman citizen. James is said to have been the ruler of a wholly Jerusalem Church, and though an early Christian retained all the outward trappings of a conscientious Jew. (The word Christ did not originally relate specifically to Jesus. It is from the Greek word 'Christos' and refers to one who is anointed. Therefore it is quite acceptable to suggest that the Ebionites believed in a Christ, which simply means an anointed leader.)

If circumstances had been different it is possible that the Jerusalem branch of Christianity may have come to be the accepted version of the faith. However, just prior to 70 AD the Jews of Judaea, incensed at the treatment they received from their Roman overlords, and having long planned the event, rose up against Rome. The revolt was handled very well and at first it looked as though the Romans would lose command of the area. However, the Emperor sent more legions to Judaea and eventually the rebellion was crushed with the most awful cruelty.

It was at this time that the famous Temple in Jerusalem, originally built by Solomon, was destroyed. In fact it was just nearing completion after a third rebuild, on this occasion by the Roman puppet king, Herod. The destruction of the Temple was a deliberate act on the part of the forces of Rome, who recognised the building as a rallying point and centre of opposition to Roman rule.

In the atrocities that followed the Jewish uprising the Romans made no distinction between Jews and Christians, and in fact may have been deeply suspicious of the new sect. It is impossible to say what happened to the Ebionite communities or those of the Essene. However, the Muslim historian, Abd al Jabbar, encountered the Ebionites as late as 1000 AD and groups of Ebionites were said to be living further east, in two communities, the names of which are unidentifiable (Theyma and Thilmes), as late as 1100 AD. Ebionite survival at this period is also validated by the Jewish Rabbi, Benjamin of Tudela in his *Book of the Travels*. It has further been suggested that groups of Ebionites may have underpinned the 'Arian' conspiracy that threatened to split Christianity in its very early days. It is even proposed that the Ebionites may have played a part in the ultimate creation of Islam.

Many of the inhabitants of Judaea were either killed or sold into slavery after the 70 AD uprising but it is certain that a sizeable proportion of the population managed to escape, either during the uprising or subsequently. Presumably these escapees would have included members of the Ebionite and Essene communities and they could have eventually found their way to almost any part of the known world.

As we have noted, according to the Catholic Church and the information given by Pope Pius IX, a Johannite sect, most likely the Ebionites, was still operative in the Near East at the time of the Crusades. Pius specifically states that a continuous line of the followers of John the Baptist existed, having succeeded '*Saint John by an uninterrupted succession of pontifical power.*' He even names the successor to St John at the time the first Templar knights had arrived in the Levant. The name he quotes is 'Theoclet'. Pius asserts that Theoclet passed his position of head of the Johannite Church to Hughes de Payen, who was a founder member and first leader of the Knights Templar.

So, the Ebionites were heretical in the eyes of the established Church and saw themselves as Jewish, though more in its ancient Enochian than first century sense. They disbelieved the stories of the Virgin Birth and Jesus' position as Messiah and they were staunch followers of John the Baptist. Even more startling was the fact that the Ebionites responded to only one book, which they viewed as their prime biblical document. This was the Hebrew version of St Matthew.

Meanwhile, and almost fifteen hundred years later, we were faced with Rosslyn Chapel. We had shown conclusively, and as far as we could tell for the first time, that Rosslyn Chapel was built, at least partly, as a direct and obvious response to an old legend relating to St Matthew, the saint for whom the chapel had been named. Stories concerning the chapel are replete with mentions of the Knights Templar and also Freemasonry, and both these institutions had held, and in the case of Freemasonry still holds, a reverence for St John the Baptist.

Despite our original reticence to involve ourselves in legends, the information at our disposal seemed to point to the fact that there might indeed be a very real connection between Rosslyn Chapel, the Knights Templar and the later Freemasons. What we needed were tangible connections between the Ebionites of the 1st century and events in Europe that had ultimately led to the emergence of groups such as the Templars and Cistercians, and finally to the building of Rosslyn Chapel. As it turned out, we already had them.

The hidden imperative

In a previous book, *The Goddess, the Grail and the Lodge*, Alan had shown that there were direct connections between the Jerusalem Church at the start of the modern era and groups such as the Knights Templar. These became most evident in Europe with a series of events that took place between the late 11th and late 13th century, all of which related to the more or less independent region of Champagne, now part of modern France.

Alan showed that Essene and Ebionite Jews escaping from the chaos caused by the Jewish uprising of 70 AD had travelled to Southern France. There they had prospered and had married into some of the ruling families that developed after the fall of the Roman Empire in the 6th century. With the passing of centuries they became most noticeable in Burgundy and Champagne, and it was from the latter of these regions that surviving Jerusalem Church followers began to plan a way by which they could regain Jerusalem and re-instate the form of Christianity to which they still tenaciously clung. The Pauline Christian Church, based in Rome, had remained all-powerful, so the surviving Ebionites could not espouse their beliefs openly. Rather they had to bide their time and plan carefully, all the time gaining influence, not only within society but also at the very heart of the Church.

Their moment came in 1088 when a man called Odo of Lagery, an individual born of aristocratic parents and directly related to the Count of

Troyes Cathedral, Champagne. Troyes was the centre of political and religious revolutions from the 11th to the early 14th centuries

Champagne, was made Pope. Odo took the name Urban II and he soon publicly appealed for a great crusade that could free the Holy Land, and Jerusalem in particular, from Muslim domination.

At the same time as the First Crusade was taking place, largely led by aristocrats from Champagne, there were other developments. Robert of Molesmes was born of aristocratic parents in Champagne in 1029. Robert was a Benedictine monk who founded and became abbot of the monastery of Molesmes in Champagne. Keen to stick more rigidly to the most primitive form of Benedictine monasticism possible, he moved from Molesmes in 1098, together with a small band of brothers, to found a new abbey in Northern Burgundy. The new abbey was built on land granted by the Duke of Burgundy, a man blood tied to the Count of Champagne.

The monks settled at Citeaux and soon became known as Cistercians, a name that was given to them on account of the huge water cisterns they dug at Citeaux. In almost every respect the new order was a modern, Christian counterpart of the Jewish Essene brotherhood, a sect closely tied to the Ebionites that had flourished in sites such as Qumran in the Jordan Valley in the decades running up the modern era. Like the Essenes of old the Cistercians wore white, deliberately built their abbeys in wild

Citeaux Abbey, Burgundy. Mother house of the Cistercian order of Monks since the 12th century

and desolate places, were vegetarians and washed regularly (which definitely wasn't common in the 12th century.) Also like the Essene the Cistercians embraced poverty and common property, were run in a democratic way, espoused a belief in the creation of God's kingdom on Earth and shunned society whenever possible.

The Cistercians carved out a small niche for themselves at Citeaux, gradually growing in numbers and refining their order at the same time as Christian control was being established across the Holy Land. Jerusalem had been captured by the Crusaders in 1099 and soon afterwards was being ruled by a Christian king, a man from the same tightly knit group of Northern French aristocrats ruling Champagne.

Portrait of St Bernard of Clairvaux from the treasury of Troyes Cathedral, Champagne, France

In 1112 yet another Champagne aristocrat, this one called Bernard, a cousin of the Count of Champagne, arrived at the gates of Citeaux with thirty of his family members and retainers. Bernard did not simply join the Cistercian order. Together with his followers he swamped it. Three years later Bernard had his own Cistercian abbey, at Clairvaux (The Valley of Holy Light) in Champagne, only a few short miles from Troyes, Champagne's capital and the place where the Count kept his court. Under Bernard's excellent guidance the Cistercians began to expand rapidly, founding abbeys across Champagne, Burgundy, Normandy and also in Britain.

It was in 1118, three years after the founding of Clairvaux, that Hugh de Payen travelled from Troyes to Jerusalem with eight companions. Hugh himself was yet another kinsman of the Champagne Count and his immediate second-in-command was Andre de Montbard, the brother of Bernard's mother. Their avowed intent (at least publicly) was to protect the roads of the Holy Land for pilgrims but there is no evidence that they ever did anything of the sort. Rather they spent the next few years garrisoned in the stables on the Temple Mount in Jerusalem, directly over the ruins of the old Temple. According to Masonic legends they were busy digging for 'something' that they clearly knew had been hidden there prior to the last destruction of the Temple by the Romans.

Whilst the first Templar knights were busy in Jerusalem, and Bernard of Clairvaux was gaining power and influence within the Church, another plan was taking shape. Hugh, the Count of Champagne, suddenly and quite mysteriously resigned his offices and left his entire inheritance to his nephew Thibaud, who in 1125 became Count Thibaud II of Champagne. Hugh set sail for the Near East, joining Hugh de Payen and the other Templar knights in Jerusalem. There, in a reversal of roles, Hugh of Champagne became a vassal of Hugh de Payen.

Upon coming to power Thibaud, the new Count of Champagne, immediately embarked on a strategy that would make Champagne far richer and more powerful than any of the surrounding regions. He created a series of international gatherings, known as the Champagne Fairs. These took place in various locations within Champagne across the entire year. Their purpose was simple. Merchants from all over Europe and beyond came together at the Champagne Fairs in order to trade. Champagne was ideally situated for this purpose and with Thibaud's excellent handling the Champagne Fairs began to prosper and grow very quickly.

The capture of large areas of the Near East by Western forces had opened up trade routes from the Middle East and far beyond. Luxury goods, such as silk and spices, that had previously been difficult if not impossible to source now became available. These began to find their way along sea routes from the far end of the Mediterranean to the southern ports of France. From there they were transhipped up to Champagne, where they met other goods coming from further north. Thibaud offered security of passage to merchants from many different places and gave them warehousing and safe accommodation. He made sure that the exchange of money became possible and introduced new currency and common units of weights and measures. But none of this would have been of use if the European merchants had nothing to trade for the exotic goods arriving in Champagne.

It was the Cistercians who came up with the answer. From the very outset they had made themselves into admirable farmers, with a particular interest in sheep rearing. The Cistercians were not interested in the meat from their sheep, because they were vegetarians. Rather they wanted the sheeps' wool.

In Flanders, a geographical area taking in much of the modern Netherlands, parts of Belgium and Northern France, the locals already had a good expertise in cleaning, spinning and weaving wool into good cloth. Some of the earliest Cistercian abbeys had been located in Flanders and there the monks had concentrated on draining vast areas of marshy, sea-washed land, the better to make room for great herds of sheep. The wool from these early Cistercian flocks was sold to the spinners and weavers of Flanders who transformed it. The finished bales of cloth were than taken down to Champagne to be traded for goods coming from the East.

The weavers of Flanders soon became so efficient that there were never enough sheep on their own land to satisfy the demand for raw wool, but the Cistercians had the answer. They began to found abbeys in England, Scotland and Wales, where they ran even larger herds of sheep than had been possible anywhere on the Continent. The wool from Britain was transhipped to Flanders, in order to feed the ever-multiplying looms, and the resulting cloth added to that being traded in Champagne. Secular landowners and farmers soon realised that sheep were easy to rear and that they could be very profitable. As a result Britain became famous for its excellent long-staple wool.

The first Templar knights came back from Jerusalem in 1128, after a stay of nine years. By the time they returned Bernard of Clairvaux was rocketing to a position of influence and authority within the Church. Bernard persuaded the Pope, Honorius II, to convene a great Church Council in Troyes, capital of Champagne, and further convinced the Pope to make the Knights Templars into a fully-fledged order of fighting monks, officially sanctioned and, on paper at least, responsible to no other authority than that of the Pope himself. It was at this time that 'The Poor Fellow Soldiers of Christ and the Temple of Solomon' became a legitimate monastic order.

Henceforth the meteoric rise of the Cistercians was quickly matched by that of the Templars. Like their Cistercian brothers the Templars wore white and the rule by which they lived was written by Bernard of Clairvaux. It was a virtual replica of the Cistercian's own rule of conduct. The Templars were supposed to exist to fight Muslims in the Holy Land but they very quickly became much more than holy soldiers. They built a powerful navy and began to indulge in trade. They also became excellent builders, creating not just military bases but farms, villages, towns and ports, the better to support their rapidly growing empire. Like the Cistercians the Templars became great sheep farmers, but unlike their cousins, who were tied to their abbeys, the Templars could travel wherever they wished. Although there were many Templars in the Near East, who fought with great courage and enterprise, the base of the Templar Empire remained in Troyes. There they became essential to the Champagne Fairs. The Templars were the first Christians to become financiers and bankers, created great networks of credit transactions and soon grew very, very rich.

There was one further Champagne-inspired action around this time, and this was the founding of another reformed Benedictine order of monks. Similar in many ways to the Cistercians this order, somewhat confusingly started by another Bernard, built its Mother abbey in 1109 on land near to Chartres, a city ruled by the Counts of Champagne. The Order's first abbey had been at Thiron and so the monks soon came to be known as Tironensians. Just as surely as the Cistercians were sheep farmers, the Tironensians were builders. From the very inception of the order Bernard of Thiron gathered together all the craftsmen he could persuade to join the infant order, bringing together the best stonemasons to be found in France and beyond. Despite being almost missing from the historical record the Tironensian order was phenomenally successful and very quickly established over a hundred monasteries, some of the earliest of which were in Scotland.

Around 1130 the Count of Champagne prevailed upon the Tironensian monks to found a School of Architecture in Chartres and it may well have been there that the Templars gained some of their own acumen in advanced building techniques. The existence of the Tironensians, and the strong presence they soon established in Scotland would ultimately contribute to the building of Rosslyn Chapel.

Seen chronologically, we have the following sequence of events, which appear linked.

1. The creation of a Champagne-born Pope and the call for a Crusade to free Jerusalem.
2. The creation of the Cistercians by another high-ranking Champagne aristocrat.
3. Bernard of Clairvaux's entry into the Cistercian order and his meteoric rise within the Church.

4. The influence of the Cistercians in Flanders and their rapid rise as large-scale sheep farmers.
5. The departure of the nine monks from Champagne to Jerusalem in 1118.
6. The creation of the Tironensian order of monks on Champagne-owned land at Chartres and the founding of the School of architecture there around 1130.
7. The creation by the Count of Champagne of the Champagne Fairs.
8. The return of the first Templar Knights to Champagne in 1128, where thanks to the influence of Bernard of Clairvaux they became an officially sanctioned military religious order.
9. The growth of the Cistercians, the Tironensians and the Knights Templar, the raison d'etre of each dovetailing into that of the others, providing the means by which trade in Western Europe was transformed. This ultimately lead to an erosion of feudal rule and loss of power on the part of the established Catholic Church.

The Sinclairs who built Rosslyn Chapel had originated in the very same part of Northern France from which all these imperatives had also come. Their very name, originally St Clair, means 'The Holy Shining Light'. The Sinclairs had always been on good terms with both the Cistercians and the Tironensians and both orders maintained abbeys on Sinclair land. Could it be possible that Earl William Sinclair was a member of a family that had maintained its Ebionite, Jewish roots across fourteen hundred years of history? The evidence being presented by Rosslyn Chapel seemed to indicate that this could indeed be the case.

7

The Shekinah

WITH REGARD TO Rosslyn Chapel itself the time had come to take stock. We now knew, at least in part, why the rich ornamentation of Rosslyn Chapel looks the way it does. We had uncovered the story of St Matthew and his magical staff and we knew that this tale was certainly in circulation during the 15th century. No visiting Church dignitary could possibly have found fault with what he saw at Rosslyn Chapel when it appeared to echo so well this important story regarding St Matthew, who was after all the patron saint of the chapel. However, we were equally certain that there was far more to the carvings than even this tale could afford.

We had to bear in mind that all the available evidence showed that the construction of Rosslyn Chapel, at least above ground, probably did not start until 1456 because this was the time Earl William Sinclair had quitted his appointments at Court, when he came into a significant amount of money, and when he had also achieved borough status for his new village. It was also the year in which Sir Gilbert Haye is reported as having returned to Scotland.

Almost casually Alan, who is a lifelong expert in both astronomy and astrology, took a look at the heavens over Rosslyn as they would have appeared on St Matthew's Day in this crucial year of 1456. What he discovered came as a surprise.

Where God dwells

Associated with the very early days of Hebrew history is a common and reccurring theme that has, for as much as 3,000 years, taxed the brains of Jewish historians and intellectuals. This is the constant reference within Jewish tradition to something known as the 'Shekinah.' The Shekinah in its Old Testament sense referred to phenomena in which the presence of God could be seen acting in some physical way, such as the column of cloud that led the Children of Israel through the wilderness during the day and the pillar of fire that guided them by night.

The Shekinah was also said to be the presence of God within the Holy of Holies – that part of the Jerusalem Temple where the Ark of the Covenant was kept. Looking way back into Enochian literature and at the earliest records of Jewish history and mysticism, the authors Knight and Lomas had begun to recognise within the Shekinah a cosmological happening – something that created an intense light, close the horizon, very rarely and then only at specific times of day.[11] Enlisting Alan's astronomical expertise and reducing the possibilities one by one it became apparent that the physical manifestation of the Shekinah in the sky over Jerusalem could have been only one thing – a conjunction (coming together) of the planets Mercury and Venus just before dawn.

Knight and Lomas showed that immediately beyond the Ark of the Covenant in the Holy of Holies in the Jerusalem Temple had been a portal or window, with an uninterrupted view of the eastern horizon. The two golden angels fixed to the top of the Ark had wings that arched up and converged in such a way that the portal stood in the space between their wings and the top of the Ark. Thus anything that appeared in the portal would, to the observer, seem to stand above the Ark, framed by the angel's wings. What they awaited with anticipation was the Shekinah. This was seen as being a manifestation of the conjoining of the male and female components of Godhead – a power that came from above together with God's manifestation from the Ark that created the holy communion between Earth and Heaven in the space between the outstretched wings of the golden angels.

The planets Mercury and Venus both lie within the orbit of the Earth. Mercury in particular is very close to the sun and so, from an earthbound

---

11   Christopher Knight and Robert Lomas, *The Book of Hiram*, Century, London, 2003

The Earl's Pillar, known to Freemasons as the Masters Pillar

To the left is the Earl's Pillar and to the right is the pillar known to Freemasons as the Journeyman's Pillar

The Great East Window of Rosslyn Chapel, showing the Light Box in the point of the arch

View of Rosslyn Chapel from the East, showing the crypt in the foreground

The Princes Pillar, known to Freemasons as the Apprentice Pillar

Alternative view of the Princes Pillar

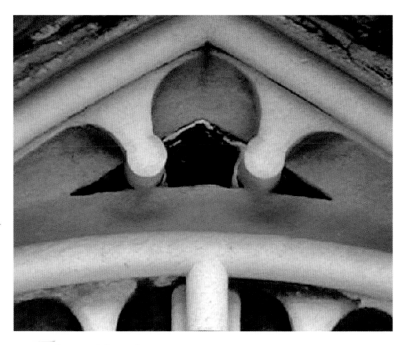

External view of the Light Box

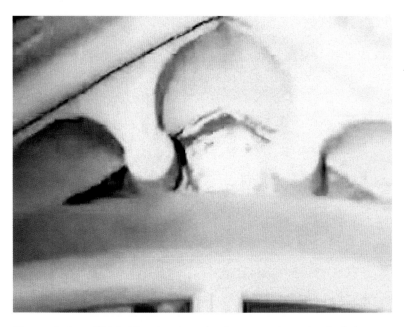

External view of Light Box showing what happens when a bright light is shone into the aperture

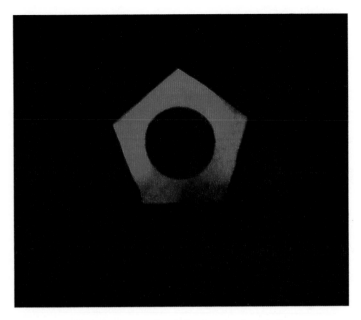

The recreated Light Box with a light shining from below

The recreated Light Box with a light shining directly from behind

View from the Chapel

Rosslyn Castle seen through the trees

perspective, it never seems to wander far from the sun in the sky. This makes it very difficult to see and it is only visible with the naked eye at very specific times, either immediately before dawn, or immediately after sunset, dependent on which side of the sun it happens to be as seen from Earth. The orbit of Venus stands between that of Mercury and the Earth. Venus is seen from the Earth like Mercury, as either a morning or an evening star but unlike Mercury it is capable of rising as much as three hours before the sun or setting as much as three hours after it.

Venus has always been one of the most mysterious and fascinating planets, because it shines so bright in our night sky (in fact it can often be seen in daylight if one knows where to look) and keeps the strangest imaginable mathematical relationship with the Earth. The orbital period of Venus (as seen from Earth and so not its actual orbital period) is 584 days, whilst that of the Earth is 365 days. This means that eight Earth years is equal to almost exactly five Venus cycles. Venus has almost always been recognised as a feminine planet and has been equated with specific goddesses by numerous cultures. It still carries the name of a goddess because Venus was a Roman deity and the equivalent of the Greek Goddess Aphrodite.

In order to be seen from the Earth, the Shekinah, which occurs when the planets Mercury and Venus stand absolutely side-by-side in the sky, can only happen a short while before dawn. Although meetings of the two bodies are common, the vast majority of them take place during daylight on Earth and so cannot be seen with the naked eye. Only under very rare circumstances is the Shekinah observable from any particular point on the Earth, and even then, for it to look really potent and impressive, the two planets must occupy almost the same point in the sky horizontally as well as vertically. This is even rarer. When seen on a clear morning before dawn the close conjunction of Mercury and Venus appears on the horizon as a very bright, white light. It increases in intensity as the sun rises immediately below the horizon and then turns blood red as the first fingers of the rising sun begin to creep across the horizon. It then disappears into the full power of the risen sunlight.

The Hebrews had observed the Holy Shekinah around the year 1448 BC, and it had heralded the building of Solomon's Temple in Jerusalem. Because such events maintain a repeatable and predictable pattern, the Shekinah had been looked for again, 1,440 years later, in 8 BC. This was the time when a new Messiah was expected to arise – a man who would free the Jews from the yoke of Roman oppression and whose presence would herald the new Jerusalem that was expected to be God's kingdom of Earth.

The Shekinah had duly arrived on 21 December 8 BC, most probably around the time of the birth of John the Baptist or Jesus. Contrary to popular belief neither Jesus or his near contemporary John can have been born in 1 AD.[12] But although the Shekinah arrived as predicted the New Jerusalem did not come about. For decades the Jews fought tenaciously to fulfil the words of the prophets and free their land from slavery, but after 70 AD their dreams fell in tatters as Rome annihilated hundreds of thousands of Jews and utterly destroyed the sacred Temple.

Those Ebionites who survived the destruction of Jerusalem and who came to prosper and flourish in distant lands, if they had maintained their ages-old traditions, would have expected another Shekinah to take place on 21 December 1432 AD. If so they were disappointed, because the Shekinah did not appear on that date. The reason for its absence lies in the fact that although the solar system is a wonderful clock and Venus is an excellent minute hand on that clock, such long-lived astronomical patterns do eventually decay. By 1432 AD both Venus and Mercury were too close to the sun for the Shekinah to be seen.

Formerly, in 1448 BC and 8 BC the Shekinah had been expected to arrive on the day of the winter solstice – that time of the year when the sun rises far south of east and one of the most potent and important dates in the ancient calendar. By the 15th century, mainly thanks to the efforts of Arab astronomers, star watching was far more advanced than it had been around the time of the birth of Jesus. Anyone who had the requisite skills (and we can be certain that Sir Gilbert Haye was such a person), would have been able to work out when the Shekinah would be seen again. He would have eventually realised that the Shekinah had switched its allegiance from the winter solstice to another one of the four corner days of the year, and this time it would appear at the Autumn Equinox, in the year 1456. This Shekinah is what was displayed on the planetarium screen of Alan's astronomical programme for the date in question and part of the screen is reproduced below.

---

12 According to the Bible King Herod was alive when Jesus was born but was dead before 1 AD.

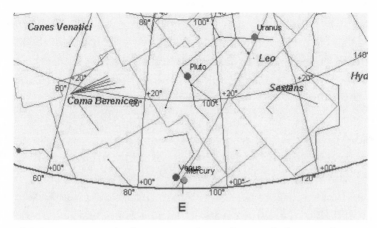

The planetarium picture for 6am on 21 September 1456 looking east from Rosslyn just before dawn. The letter 'E' represents East, whilst the bottom curved line is the horizon. Mercury and Venus, appearing in the form of the Holy Shekinah can be seen just above the eastern horizon. Their combined light would have made them appear as one coherent and very bright light

So rare is this astronomical occurrence that the thought of it happening by chance on 21 September, St Matthew's Day, in the same tight time period that Rosslyn Chapel was built would be a breathtaking coincidence. Venus and Mercury would not appear at the Autumn Equinox again for many, many generations! It is partly for this reason but also on chronological grounds that we believe this was the day on which the cornerstone of Rosslyn Chapel was laid, fully in accordance with procedures that had been practised since truly ancient times.

Not only was St Matthew's feast day on 21 September, a date that had been of crucial religious importance since time out of mind, but work on the actual fabric of the chapel seemed to have been delayed until a moment that we knew would have been very auspicious, not only to the ancient Hebrews but to those who had retained its deepest and most sacred traditions. This date in September was also the Autumn Equinox – the time of harvest and sacrifice and the period at which the Corn God gives up his life to feed humanity.

There already seemed to be significant evidence to substantiate that there was a direct and intended connection between the Temple in Jerusalem and the building of Rosslyn Chapel. This was borne out by the appearance of the Shekinah, which itself was associated with both the first and second Jerusalem Temples. Although it seemed likely that permission to build the Chapel had been obtained as early as 1440, we could see for a number of equally valid and provable reasons that work on the fabric of the building had been delayed for some reason, most likely to do with the Shekinah.

However, we do not suggest that the site of the chapel was standing idle prior to this time. Extensive excavations would have been necessary for such an undertaking and if rumours of a subterranean vault are to be believed these may have taken years to complete. Such work would have had to be finished before the first stone of the chapel proper could be laid and it is possible that the excavations had been underway for a decade or more prior to 1456.

Our next task was to look more closely at the Shekinah, because although its most important cosmological association was the conjunction before dawn of the planets Mercury and Venus, there was much more to this mysterious and important subject that its manifestation in the sky.

The word Shekinah derives from the Hebrew word 'Shachan', which literally means 'to reside'. All agencies agree that the feminisation of this word, making it 'Shekinah', came to mean something truly important to the Jews from their most ancient times. It appears that the Shekinah originally meant the presence of God within the community of Israel. The expression, 'the Shekinah rests' was used as a paraphrase or euphemism for 'God Dwells'.

The word Shekinah is not actually used in the Old Testament because it only came into use around the first or second centuries of the modern era, though the essence of what Shekinah would come to mean is to be found in the words and actions of the prophets Elijah and Ezekiel, and it is suggested that the Shekinah was present and a strong influence during moments of great import to the early Jewish story. Where the Shekinah really comes into its own is in the 'Kabala', which is alternatively spelt Cabbala and Kabbalah.

The Kabala

The Kabala is a work of the utmost importance, not only to Judaism but also to developing Christianity. It is nothing more or less than the combined mystical teachings of Judaism, some parts of which are thought to be extremely old, even though they may not have been committed to the written word until well into the modern era. At its simplest the Kabala attempts to explain God's purpose in Creation, as well as to throw light on the most important rules to which Jewish people still adhere, namely the Torah. The Kabala is not simply one book but represents a whole canon of literature. It is fiercely complicated and goes into great detail about the minutia of God's Creation – not merely at a level that is open to human perception, but also with regard to layers of spirits and angels that are said to inhabit realms both above and below those occupied by humanity.

The Kabala also attempts to explain the world in a physical sense, so much so that both Arabic and Christian scholars drew heavily on its material in the creation of their own canons of mysticism. In its most practical aspect, study of the Kabala ultimately grew into 'alchemy', which in turn is the direct parent of chemistry and which, despite its fantastic components, genuinely did contribute to eventual scientific knowledge.

Is this the angel Earl William Sinclair and Sir Gilbert Haye recognised as the Angel of the Shekinah?

A major component of the Kabala is a book known as the 'Zohar'. It first appeared in its written form in 13th century Spain, thanks to the work of a Jewish Rabbi named Moses ben Shem Tov de Leon. Shem Tov claimed that the Zohar had been passed to him as an oral tradition and maintained it had first come about in the second century of the modern era and was ultimately the work of another Rabbi, Simeon ben Yohai. The Zohar shot to popularity within a few short years of its appearance.

The Zohar is not one work but many, all brought together by Moses de Leon and it now also contains explanations and commentaries by later influential Jewish Rabbis and mystics. The name Zohar means 'splendour' and 'radiance'. It represents a mystical interpretation of the Torah, which is the canon of books that comprises Jewish law and custom. The purpose of the Zohar is to examine God and his creation from a mystical standpoint. It describes the origin and structure of the universe, together with the nature of the human soul and offers advice on life, death, sin and redemption.

It is within the Zohar that we discover so much about the Shekinah, not in its cosmological manifestation, but rather as a spiritual entity that is so close to Godhead that it may as well be considered an integral part of the supreme Deity. The Zohar tells us that the Shekinah is 'the angel of justice' and the 'bride of God' but it is also much more. According to the Zohar the creation of the world in a material sense was the work of the Shekinah. The apparent reason for this is because God himself is so elevated, so remote and unapproachable, that only through the intermediary of the Shekinah can his divine thoughts be made manifest in the world.

Interestingly enough the Zohar refers to the Shekinah as being 'the way of the Tree of Life'. The Kabala sees the different levels of existence, both material and spiritual, as being a great tree with many branches. The Shekinah is said to sit at the base of this tree, willingly dwelling amongst humanity, but with contact to all the other spiritual agencies above, and also to God Himself.

The Shekinah appears to be close, both linguistically and in character, to an agency from a different and almost certainly even older source, namely Hinduism. In Hindu mythology and religion one of the most important deities is Shiva. Shiva is a capricious God. Like the God of the Zohar he is distant, unconcerned, unconventional and unpredictable. His creative potential for humanity is crucial but it can only be made manifest

The Kabalistic Tree of Life

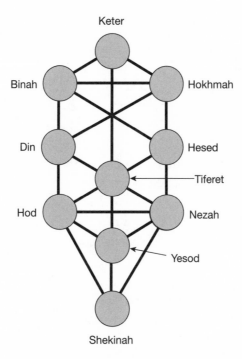

Each of the globes represent Sefirot.
These are connected by pathways.

in the world thanks to his 'Shakti'. Shakti is the active manifest power that created and continues to create the universe. Shakti is female and is the counterpart in every way of the more remote Shiva. In mythological stories the Shakti of Shiva is often named 'Parvati'. She holds a very important place in Hinduism because it is said that without her creative potential the corporeal universe would not have resulted.

Parvati, as Shakti, is the caring, attentive wife. Shiva is aesthetic and cares little for procreation or family. But without procreation the potential of the universe as we perceive it cannot be born into reality. Parvati coaxes and woos Shiva and is generally depicted as being a willing friend to humanity and to nature as a whole.

Although there are differences pointed out by experts, there is clearly an important connection between the Shakti of Hindu religion and the Shekinah of Hebrew ancestry – in fact we would go so far as to say that there may be a direct historical relationship, and if so this goes back to the dawn of humanity, since Hinduism is based on some of the very oldest religious imperatives of our species.

In the Kabala and in particular the Zohar, the Shekinah is described as being surrounded by sixty or more guardian angels. Some legends assert that when Adam and Eve were banished from the Garden of Eden the Shekinah remained behind, seated at the base of the Tree of Life where her splendour was 65,000 times the radiance of the sun. Other stories suggest that she accompanied Adam and Eve and that the very purpose of the Torah (the sacred law) is to lead the Shekinah back to God. It is further suggested that after the fall of man, the Shekinah gradually retreated further and further up the Tree of Life, eventually gaining the 7th heaven. She was only coaxed back to earth by the actions of seven wise men. These were Abraham, Issac, Joseph, Jacob, Levi, Kehath and Moses.

The Zohar insists that the Shekinah is, at one and the same time the sister, wife and mother of God, though this fact is never specifically mentioned in the Old Testament of the Bible. In this form it represents more modern interpretations – though it has to be stressed that these extend far back in time, at least to the commencement of the modern era.

The inscription

According to Jewish traditions the Shekinah resided in the Holy of Holies within the Temple, specifically within or close to the Ark of the Covenant. Her position there was of the utmost importance because the Israelite communion with God could not be complete without her presence. When the Temple of Solomon was destroyed by King Nebuchadnezzar and his Babylonian army, (around 600 BC), the Shekinah was driven from Jerusalem. In other words she could no longer reside with the Jews and thus their special communion with God was broken. What followed was a long period of exile for most of the Israelites in Babylon.

Seventy years later the King of Babylon agreed to allow the Jews to return to Jerusalem and he even returned to them the treasure that his predecessor had looted from the Temple. At this time, possibly around 500 BC, a second Temple was completed and, according to Kabalistic and Jewish tradition, the Shekinah returned to Jerusalem and the communion with God was restored.

*The only inscription in Rosslyn Chapel.
In translation from Latin it reads: 'Wine
is strong, the king is stronger, women are
stronger still but the truth is strongest of all'*

It was at this time that the story arose which ultimately led to the only inscription to be found in Rosslyn Chapel. This is the Latin inscription over the door to the crypt, which in translation reads. 'Wine is strong, the King is stronger, women are stronger still but truth is the strongest of all.'

It relates to the period at the end of the Babylonian captivity and to a Jewish bodyguard of the Babylonian King Darius by the name of Zerubbabel. Together with two other bodyguards, Zerubbabel was called into the king's presence. For the sake of diversion the king gave each of his bodyguards a word or words and asked them to debate which of these was the strongest. These were wine, the king, and women and truth. The first bodyguard dealt with wine and suggested that it was the strongest because it robbed men of their senses. The second bodyguard discussed the power of the King, suggesting that through his might he was stronger by far than wine. When Zerubbabel spoke he pointed out the power of women in every part of society. However, he ultimately decided that truth was the strongest of all. According to the historian Josephus Zerubbabel said:

> *Now when this man had held his peace the third of them, who was
> Zerubbabel, began to instruct them about women, and about truth,
> who said thus: "Wine is strong, as is the king also, whom all men obey,
> but women are superior to them in power; for it was a woman that
> brought the king into the world; and for those that plant the vines and
> make the wine, they are women who bear them, and bring them up: nor
> indeed is there any thing which we do not receive from them; for these
> women weave garments for us, and our household affairs are by their
> means taken care of, and preserved in safety; nor can we live separate
> from women. And when we have gotten a great deal of gold and silver,
> and any other thing that is of great value, and deserving regard, and see*

a beautiful woman, we leave all these things, and with open mouth fix our eyes upon her countenance, and are willing to forsake what we have, that we may enjoy her beauty, and procure it to ourselves. We also leave father, and mother, and the earth that nourishes us, and frequently forget our dearest friends, for the sake of women; nay, we are so hardy as to lay down our lives for them. But what will chiefly make you take notice of the strength of women is this that follows: Do not we take pains, and endure a great deal of trouble, and that both by land and sea, and when we have procured somewhat as the fruit of our labours, do not we bring them to the women, as to our mistresses, and bestow them upon them? Nay, I once saw the king, who is lord of so many people, smitten on the face by Apame, the daughter of Rabsases Themasius, his concubine, and his diadem taken away from him, and put upon her own head, while he bore it patiently; and when she smiled he smiled, and when she was angry he was sad; and according to the change of her passions, he flattered his wife, and drew her to reconciliation by the great humiliation of himself to her, if at my time he saw her displeased at him."

And when the princes and rulers looked one upon another, he began to speak about truth; and he said, "I have already demonstrated how powerful women are; but both these women themselves, and the king himself, are weaker than truth; for although the earth be large, and the heaven high, and the course of the sun swift, yet are all these moved according to the will of God, who is true and righteous, for which cause we also ought to esteem truth to be the strongest of all things, and that what is unrighteous is of no force against it. Moreover, all things else that have any strength are mortal and short-lived, but truth is a thing that is immortal and eternal. It affords us not indeed such a beauty as will wither away by time, nor such riches as may be taken away by fortune, but righteous rules and laws. It distinguishes them from injustice, and puts what is unrighteous to rebuke." [13]

Josephus goes on to report that as a result of his eloquent words, King Darius allowed Zerubbabel to take the families of the Jewish captives and to return to Jerusalem, where it is said he began building the second Temple.

---

13 Josephus, The Antiquities of the Jews. Book 2, Chapter 3

Although the second Temple was, at a later date, much enlarged by Herod, around the time of Jesus, this intended third Temple was never fully completed. After the Jewish uprising of 70 AD the Temple was utterly destroyed. It was at this time therefore that the Jews were dispersed and no new Temple was ever built on the original mound. What stands there today, though on the original platform of the Jewish Temple, is an Islamic Mosque.

The Beloved

Some followers of the Jewish Kabala believe that though Jews are now dispersed around the world and the Temple no longer exists, the Shekinah can still be called upon. It is suggested that the Shekinah is invoked during the preparations for the Sabbath. To many Jews the Sabbath and the Shekinah are synonymous and both represent the 'bride of God'. Hence the following Sabbath hymn, which is still sung by Jews around the world. It is called "L'cha Doedee":

Come my beloved to welcome the bride, the presence of Shabbat we receive.

"Observe and Remember" in one divine utterance, we heard from the One and Only god, the Lord is One, and His Name One, for renown, for splendor, and for praise. Come my beloved.

Shake off the dust, arise! Dress in garments of glory, my people, through the son of Jesse, the Bethlehemite, redemption draws near to my soul. Come my beloved.

Wake up, wake up! For your light has come, awaken, awaken, sign a song, for the glory of the Lord is revealed to you! Come my beloved.

The 'beloved' is both the Shekinah and the Sabbath and this hymn runs very close to the theme of a strange book from the Old Testament that is called 'Solomon's Song of Songs' or 'The Song of Solomon'. Ostensibly the Song of Solomon has little to do with religion because it appears to be a song of love, sung between a bride and a bridegroom. It is filled with wonderful poetic phrases, in which the bride and bridegroom verbalise their deep devotion, one to the other. To many of the Jewish persuasion it is clear that the Bridegroom and Bride represent God and the Shekinah. Solomon's Song of Songs represented a near obsession to Bernard of Clairvaux, the leading light of the Cistercians and a man who was undoubtedly a closet Ebionite.

It was the Shekinah, alternatively known as the Holy Spirit or the 'Sophia' that was called down when John the Baptist baptised Jesus in the waters of the River Jordan. It appeared in the form of a Dove and settled on Jesus – inferring that Jesus now shared a special 'communion' with God. One might reasonably ask the question, why was this necessary if Jesus was 'already'

Fresco of the Baptism of Jesus by John the Baptist. Note the dove at the top of the picture, representative of the Holy Spirit and the Shekinah. Fresco by Fra Angelico 1441

the Son of God? The answer is that the whole episode predates the 4rd century decision, made at a great church gathering in Nicea, that Jesus must henceforth be considered 'as one' with God – in other words of the same substance as God. In the Hebrew or Aramaic version of the Gospel of St Matthew, the inference of this event is that the 'Shekinah', 'Sophia' or 'Holy Spirit' was not present with Jesus at his birth, but was bestowed later. After the Council of Nicea the suggestion that Jesus was not 'as one' with God became a terrible heresy, and hundreds if not thousands of people paid the price with their lives for refusing to accept Jesus' divinity from birth.

If Earl William Sinclair deliberately waited until 21 September 1456 to lay the first stone of Rosslyn Chapel because he was aware that the Shekinah would make itself visibly known on a day that was, in many other respects, considered holy, only one or two conclusions are possible.

1 Earl William Sinclair was of a family that had maintained strong Jewish overtones, or else one that had habitually practised a form of Christianity that was very much older than the sanitised version that was introduced at the Council of Nicea by the Emperor Constantine. In other words he may have been an Ebionite.

2 The Earl, most likely with the influence of his bibliophile assistant

Sir Gilbert Haye, was familiar with and gave credence to the Zohar, the most potent core of the Kabala.

Either way his beliefs were clearly heretical by the standards of his day, and he could certainly not proclaim them openly.

The Knights Templar

Let us now contrast these beliefs with what we know of the Knights Templar. We have seen that it was and still is the considered opinion of the Catholic Church hierarchy that the Templars had been infected with a Johhanite heresy from the very date of the order's foundation. Accounts of the Templar trials that followed the destruction of the Templars in 1307 seemed to back this up. There was testimony that they had defiled the cross. A young Templar recruit had reported at the trials that one of his masters had shown him a crucifix and had said to him 'Do not have too much faith in this – it is too new!' Added to this was the strange bearded head, which the Templars called Baphomet, clearly equated with the head of John the Baptist. We know that when applied to the 'Atbash Cipher' Baphomet actually means 'Sophia', which in turn is the early Christian name for the Shekinah.

It might seem odd to associate the very masculine John the Baptist with the feminine Sophia, but the words masculine and feminine become very blurred in Kabalistic terms because the writers of the Kabala make it plain that for every female, corporeal or spiritual, there is a male counterpart and vice versa. In the case of the Shekinah this is called 'Metatron'.

In the Kabala, Metatron carries all the attributes of his female counterpart, the Shekinah. Metatron was associated with the ancient Jewish patriarch Enoch, and was also a name often given to Elijah, Ezekial and, very tellingly, John the Baptist. It may well be that in the act of calling down the Shekinah, it was considered that John 'became' its counterpart, the Metatron.

All of this is very interesting, but is there anything in Rosslyn Chapel to confirm that Earl William Sinclair and his able assistant Sir Gilbert Haye were not only familiar with the Kabala and in particular the Zohar but incorporated what they knew into the fabric of the building? Indeed there is, and it is something that links the chapel not only to the ancient seeds that predate its construction, but also to the whole world of Freemasonry that arose subsequently.

8

The Three Pillars

STANDING BETWEEN THE body of Rosslyn Chapel and that area presently used as a Christian altar are the three famous pillars to which visitors are usually drawn immediately. When viewed from the west the one to the right (see color section) is variously known as the Prince's Pillar and the Apprentice Pillar. This is the pillar that was undoubtedly meant (on one level at least) to represent the great tree that grew from the magical staff of St Matthew. It is the most highly ornamented of the three pillars and is considered by many to represent the crowning glory of the stone carvers' art to be seen within the chapel.

To the left of the Prince's Pillar, and therefore the central pillar of the three, is the pillar that Freemasons refer to as 'The Journeyman Pillar'. This pillar is nowhere near as ornamented as the other two and resembles the other thirteen pillars supporting the roof of the chapel. Its base is quite plain and in fact it appears to be a fairly simple fluted pillar – that is until it reaches its capital, which represents a sophisticated, complicated and wonderfully carved knot. (See colour section)

The pillar that is on the extreme left is also a beautiful example of 15th century stone carving. Known as the 'Earl's Pillar' by those without Freemasonic connections but as 'The Master's Pillar' to Masons, it is quite different in shape than any of the others, being much squarer and carrying beautifully carved details on its sides (see colour section). Interestingly this pillar is known to have been completely covered in plaster from an unknown date. This plaster was removed in the 1830s, though why it was ever covered at all remains a mystery.

For decades in the modern era visitors have stared transfixed at these pillars, and especially at the two outer ones, trying to fathom the reasoning that went into their design. To Freemasons there is no confusion about the symbolism. The three pillars are associated with the three degrees of Freemasonry. (Degrees of Freemasonry represent stages of advancement in the Craft.) To Freemasons the Prince's Pillar is known as the Apprentice Pillar, and as such it represents the 'Entered Apprentice Degree,' which is the first degree of Freemasonry. The middle pillar is called by Freemasons 'The Journeyman Pillar' and is synonymous with the second degree of Freemasonry, more properly known these days as the 'Fellowcraft Degree'. Finally, the extreme left-hand pillar, called by Freemasons the 'Master's Pillar', relates to the third degree of Freemasonry, known as the 'Master's Degree'.

Although there are much earlier Freemasonic records in Scotland, as far as can be conclusively proved today, Freemasonry in its present form can only be traced back to the 18th century. It is true that prior to this time there were Masonic Lodges, but as far as is known these were 'operative' rather that 'speculative'. In other words Masonic Lodges prior to the 18th century were supposedly concerned only with matters pertaining to the practicalities of the stonemason's career and were a reflection of the powerful guild system that ruled stonemasonry as it did other occupations. There is certainly no historical proof that the three degrees of speculative Freemasonry existed at the time Rosslyn Chapel was planned and built. The initial inference must therefore be that the Masonic names for the three pillars in Rosslyn Chapel were attached to the pillars comparatively recently, most likely in the 18th or 19th centuries. Likewise the Masonic story relating to 'The Apprentice Pillar' must be of a later invention.

This means that the three pillars of Rosslyn are most unlikely to have been created with Freemasonry in mind, but they could quite easily owe their existence to something very much older, and what is more, something that would tie them closely to the Kabala and to the Shekinah.

Axis Mundi

A slight departure is necessary here in order to revisit the concept of the 'Tree of Life'. We have looked at the Tree of Life in connection with the Prince's Pillar and the story of St Matthew, but Matthew's creation of the wonderful tree in Myrna is only an example of what turns out to be one of the most fundamental beliefs of humanity. As a concept the World Tree exists in practically every culture across the planet, and this includes hunter-gatherer groups that have had little or no contact with other civilizations. In other words the story of the World Tree is either endemic to humanity, or else goes so far back into our past it must have evolved at a time before human beings became dispersed across the planet.

In most cases the World Tree represents a means of communication between the material world in which we live, and the spirit world that is thought by many to exist beyond our normal senses. In Animistic and Shamanistic societies specific individuals make it their business to supposedly gain access to the upper reaches of the World Tree. This is sometimes achieved with the use of hallucinogenic drugs or as a result of ecstatic dances and/or prolonged periods of fasting and meditation. The reasons for accessing the World Tree and the means by which it is achieved differ markedly from one culture to another but the important fact remains the commonality of the belief in the World Tree itself.

A single Latin phrase describes the World Tree and emphasises its importance to a host of different cultures. This is the 'Axis Mundi'. This phrase literally means that place around which the heavens revolve. Historians and anthropologists tend to assume that a belief in the World Tree spread throughout Eurasia as part of Pre-Indo-European religious patterns. In this way it could also have found its way to the New World when people crossed the Bering Straights and migrated down through North and South America.

To the Nordic peoples the World Tree was Yggdrasil. It contained nine worlds in its branches and was the theme of countless folk tales. The Tongans and Figians had 'The Tree of Speech', which resembled Yggdrasil in many ways. To the Slavs the World Tree was a great oak, a tree also revered by the ancient Celts of Western Europe. In the New World we have the Wacah Chan of the Maya, and there are dozens of other examples.

To the esoteric Western mind the World Tree is synonymous with the

Kabala, because in this form of mysticism the Tree has reached its most complex form. To many devotees of this brand of mysticism the Kabala 'is' the Tree of Life, but it has become far more complex than a simple tree with a single trunk and branches. In the Kabala the Tree of Life is comprised of three columns rather than a single trunk.

Kabalists believe that with the right knowledge and preparation, humans can eventually shed their physical body and achieve a higher consciousness, in this way coming not only to know but to be as one with the divine. The three-columned tree by which this becomes possible is also known as the 'Tree of Sephiroth'. The Sephirothic Tree contains ten orbs of bright splendour. These are arranged upon the three columns and are joined by twenty-two pathways. It is these orbs that represent the Sephiroth. The three pillars of the Tree of Life are named, from right to left, Mercy, Mildness and Severity.

Everything in the Kabala is mystically associated with the letters of the Hebrew alphabet; the Pillar of Mercy (Hebrew Kav Yamin) carries the Hebrew letter 'Shin', and is said to be the male aspect. The left pillar, that of Severity (Hebrew Kav Smol) has the Hebrew letter 'Mem', and is said to be feminine. The central pillar, that of Mildness, is arguably the most important of the three because it is neutral in gender and balances the other two. Its Hebrew letter association is 'Aleph', which means 'the breath'.

All of the pillars and the Sephiroth they contain exist to achieve one objective – to access the divine. In Jewish religion it was forbidden to utter the true name of God, because it was thought that to do so might in itself be a sin. God is infinite, eternal and boundless and the minute he is defined by a name, he is being compartmentalised and cannot be approached. So remote is God from our limited perception that we cannot possibly hope to communicate with Him, or even comprehend all that He may be. However, the Kabala says that although we cannot personally know God (Eyn Sof) we can comprehend the emanations or Sephirot that shine out from Him, and it is these Sephirot that are arranged around the Kabalistic Tree of Life.

If the three pillars at the front of Rosslyn Chapel were designed and created to represent the three pillars of the Kabalistic Tree of Life, the correct way to view them could well be, not from the body of the chapel, but from the East Window. We arrive at this conclusion because most of the feminine associations in the chapel emanate from the Prince's Pillar. This is the column closest to the Lady Altar, in close proximity to the entrance to the Crypt, with its dance of death. In addition the only 'Green Woman' in the chapel is closest to the Prince's Pillar. The Prince's Pillar would therefore rightfully be the Pillar of Severity, with its strongly feminine overtones. The Earl's Pillar should then be properly called the Pillar of Mercy, and the central pillar should rightfully be known as the Pillar of Mildness.

There is no written testimony from the builders of Rosslyn Chapel with regard to the association of the three pillars and the Kabala. It would be strange indeed if such evidence had ever existed, since an admission that the chapel had Kabalistic overtones would have led Earl William and Sir Gilbert Haye to a very speedy and unpleasant death at the hands of the Church. However, the appearance of the Shekinah in the sky at the commencement of the building certainly could point in the direction of the Kabala.

Almost paradoxically, corroboration of the Kabalistic nature of the three pillars comes to us from the direction of Freemasonry. This is evidence that seems to demonstrate that the first Freemasons knew full well what the three pillars actually represented – even if most Freemasons have forgotten now.

Faith, hope and charity

Associated with each degree in Freemasonry, Masonic Temples (where Masonic lodges hold their ceremonies) contain a number of elaborate pictures. These are known as 'Tracing Boards'. According to Masonic historians the use of Tracing Boards goes back to a time when stonemasons created scale drawings of the work they were undertaking. A common procedure was for a stonemason to cover the floor of his workshop with equally sized paving slabs, which effectively then became the squares of a giant graph. He could then sketch out scale-drawings of a particular task with chalk before actually taking himself and his tools to the site.

Most Masonic lodges have chequer-board squares on their floors, which harp back to the stonemason's scale drawings and the Tracing Boards are said to represent the same desire to plan a job before it is commenced, though in this case on large pieces of cloth laid on the floor or on wooden boards. Modern Tracing Boards have little or nothing to do with the stonemason's craft. They are painted onto wood, card or canvas and no longer lay on the floor. Tracing Boards carry letters and symbols that relate to a specific degree of Freemasonry. They were and are used as a teaching aid to those aspiring to a particular degree; their symbols and pictures being interpreted to the student by a more senior member of the Lodge.

The first degree Tracing Board (see picture below) clearly shows three pillars. Each is built in its own distinctive style. In Masonic terms the right pillar is called 'Beauty' and is a Corinthian column. The left pillar carries the name 'Strength' and is a Doric column, whilst the middle pillar is called 'Wisdom' and is an Ionic column. (The three different types of pillar relate to three styles or 'orders' of Greek architecture.)

The First Degree Tracing Board of Freemasonry

The reason the Tracing Board uses three different types of columns is said to lie in their period and function. According to W. Kirk MacNulty, a high ranking American Freemason,[14] the fact that the Pillar of Beauty is a Corinthian column is because in the classic world the Corinthian order of architecture was used for buildings dedicated to vigorous, expansive activities. The Doric, in contrast, was used for buildings in which discipline, restraint and stability were important – hence its association with the Pillar of Strength. MacNulty further suggests that the middle pillar, being an Ionic column, comes from an order of architecture midway between the other two. It was used in the construction of Temples to the Gods, particularly in Athens.

It can be noted that on the example of the First Degree Tracing Board, the central pillar is associated with a ladder, which reaches from the ground towards the bright flame with an eye at its centre, known in Masonic language as 'the Glory' and representing God. In Kabalistic terms this would be entirely appropriate because the way to access divinity is via the Shekinah, who occupies her position at the base of the central column and who is the means by which communication with the higher states, and ultimately God, is achieved. The three female figures seated on the ladder are said in Masonic explanations of the Tracing Board to represent Faith, Hope and Charity. However, in Freemasonry they are always referred to as the 'three graces', whereas Faith, Hope and Charity are more properly termed 'virtues'.

One Masonic researcher, whose work in the 19th century has been of invaluable use to us, was Robert Hewitt Brown. He was a high-ranking American Freemason and in 1882 he produced a work entitled *Stella Theology and Masonic Astronomy*[15]. This is the most authoritative work on the astronomical associations of Freemasonic practice that has ever been published. When discussing faith, hope and charity in Masonic terms, Brown detaches them from their New Testament Bible context and points to a cosmological reason for their existence in the Craft. He maintains that the ladder reaching from the base of the middle pillar also represents a journey, taken by the sun, from the Winter Solstice in December, to the

---

14 Heredom, Vol 5, 1996
15 *Stella Theology and Masonic Astronomy*, Robert Hewitt Brown, First published 1882, Republished by The Book Tree, San Diego, California, USA, 2002

Spring Equinox in March. During this time the sun passes through three zodiac signs, these being Capricorn, Aquarius and Pisces, before it arrives at the first degree of Aries.

Brown suggests that Faith refers to the faith we maintain at midwinter that the spring will come again. Hope is maintained as the sun climbs daily further north at dawn before arriving at the Spring Equinox. His explanation for Charity is that on the tracing board Charity is the personification of the Divine Love felt with the arrival of spring.

On the First Degree Tracing board, and born out by W. Kirk MacNulty's explanation, the Pillar of Beauty is on the right, the Pillar of Wisdom is in the middle and the Pillar of Strength is on the left. Thus, by a simple matter of word association the Masonic pillars appear to be reversed from those of the generally accepted Kabalistic World Tree.

The Kabala – Left = Mildness, Middle = Mercy, Right = Severity
Freemasonry – Left = Strength, Middle = Wisdom, Right = Beauty

However, when viewed from the west and therefore the body of the chapel, the pillars in Rosslyn Chapel are placed in the same order as the ones appearing in the First Degree Tracing Board of Freemasonry.

We take this to be the case because Severity is more likely to be associated with Strength, whilst Beauty is more properly paired with Mildness. MacNulty makes it plain that in his opinion there is no doubting the relationship between the Three Pillars of Freemasonry and the Three Pillars of the Kabalistic World Tree. Meanwhile, the compass positioning of the Three Pillars of Freemasonry on the Tracing Board corresponds with that of the pillars in Rosslyn Chapel. All are at the east end of the building but the outer pillars are placed to the north and south of east.

Considering the close association that has been established for nearly three centuries between Rosslyn Chapel and Freemasonry, we ought to ask ourselves whether the Three Pillars used in Freemasonry are directly modelled on the pillars at the east end of Rosslyn Chapel. The only real difference lies in the different architectural orders of the pillars on the tracing board, which are not born out by those in the Chapel. But MacNulty explains that these are merely a device to better describe the logical association and function of the Masonic pillars.

How the Kabala got to Scotland

If Earl William Sinclair and Sir Gilbert Haye were aware of the Kabala to such an extent that they represented its philosophies within the very structure of Rosslyn Chapel, it stands to reason that their knowledge of it had to come from somewhere. In this respect at least the influence of Gilbert Haye would seem to be paramount.

At the time Rosslyn Chapel was built, the Kabala was extremely popular within most European states that had enjoyed Moorish or Jewish influence. For centuries the iron grip of a powerful Church that well suited the feudal forms of government that prevailed had prevented interested parties from looking at any religious or philosophical concept that differed from its own dogmas. At the very least these had been driven underground. Interest in the Kabala was a good case in question. Where Jewish communities were allowed to flourish, particularly in Britain and France, the Kabala was kept alive and for some time had funded the work of alchemists, anxious to obtain the so-called philosopher's stone which supposedly offered the chance of immortality and untold wealth. But Christians who were seen to be dabbling in the Kabala were always in danger from the Church, unless they were powerful individuals or persons working for great men who could protect them.

By the 15th century things were beginning to change, especially in the City-State of Florence in Italy. There the peculiarities of historical twists and turns had created what can probably be seen as the first democracy to emerge since the time of Ancient Greece. Florence was growing rich, mainly from the proceeds of its flourishing woollen textile industry and its leaders were set on a course that would change forever the traditional values and beliefs that had prevailed for so long.

One family in particular is remembered as the dynasty that led Florence to a position as the founding state of the Renaissance. This was the Medici. With an origin as a family of sheep breeders the Medici began to gain

Cosimo de Medici, grandfather of the Renaissance, circa 1518

influence and power in Florence as early as 1378. However it was during the life of Cosimo de Medici (1389-1464) that the true seeds of the Renaissance were sown. For sixty years Cosimo ruled Florence, and yet he had no official title. Much of his vast wealth was spent on beautifying Florence but he was also a great patron of libraries and universities. Although steering a careful path with successive popes, Cosimo de Medici gathered together all the knowledge available from the corners of the known world. Within Florence it was possible to argue philosophy and to study science – even when it contradicted the dictates of the Church. Even the Kabala itself was open for discussion in Florence. Around the time Rosslyn Chapel was being planned Cosimo de Medici created 'The Platonic Academy', a group of influential philosophical thinkers who met regularly in Florence, and it is known that the Christian Kabala was one of the topics they discussed in detail.

Undoubtedly Gilbert Haye had been to Florence and he was certainly on good terms with known followers of the Kabala, such as Rene d'Anjou. (See Chapter 14.) Gilbert Haye, like his contemporaries understood and even probably revered the Kabala but instead of committing his knowledge to velum, together with Earl William Sinclair he wrote it in stone, contributing to the great library of knowledge that Rosslyn Chapel represents. It is most likely as a result of his inspiration that the Three Pillars of Rosslyn stand to this day as a testament to the fact that knowledge of the Kabala lay at the heart of the fantastic adornment of Rosslyn Chapel.

9

A Revolution in Rome

A S A NATION Scotland was, throughout much of its independent history, much closer to Europe than was England. Constant English claims to lands beyond the Channel set the country at odds with other nations, and particularly with France. English kings, especially those of the Norman variety, were avaricious, cruel and despotic. Not only was England invariably at odds with its closest neighbours, it also had a very turbulent relationship with Rome and with its various popes. The ultimate decision of Henry VIII to split with Roman Catholicism in the 16th century came at the end of countless difficulties experienced by successive English monarchs in trying to enforce their authority against a Church hierarchy that constantly thwarted its objectives. English kings and ultimately queens too, believed that they reigned by the will of God and that no temporal power could affect their decisions or nullify their right to the throne. By the reign of Henry VIII in the 16th century, English kings also believed that no spiritual power could transcend their own.

In Scotland the situation was very different. As early as 1320 the position of the Scottish monarchy had been made abundantly clear. It was in this year that a letter was sent to Pope John XXII, seeking his recognition of Robert the Bruce as the rightful King of Scotland and also beseeching the Holy Father to lift his censure and excommunication of the entire country.

Agreed by an assembly of the Scottish aristocracy this letter has become known to history as the 'Declaration of Arbroath'. It was made plain in the declaration that no king seeking to ally himself with another nation (England especially) would be tolerated by the Scots. In other words, and with the Bruce's agreement, there could be no 'divine right of kings' in Scotland. It was, to all intents and purposes a declaration of independence and demonstrated that if it proved to be necessary kings could be removed from power by their subjects.

As time went on Scotland's relations with successive Popes were generally good. In addition, although always casting a wary eye towards its avaricious neighbour to the south, Scotland maintained an easy relationship with virtually all Western European States and enjoyed extensive trading links that were quite independent from those maintained by England. In a word Scotland, by the 15th century, understood the meaning of 'internationalism', whilst England at this time glowered out from its own fortress, suspicious and mistrustful at the world beyond.

Pope Pius II

It was to this open, cosmopolitan country of Scotland that a man came in 1435 who probably had a great deal to do with the building of Rosslyn Chapel, at least in terms of Earl William Sinclair's ability to create the masterpiece we see today. The name of this man was Enea Silvio de' Piccolomini. He had been born in Sienna in 1405, which made him a close contemporary of Earl William Sinclair, who was born in 1410. Enea was the eldest son born into a noble family made somewhat poor because he had seventeen siblings. Despite the circumstances surrounding his childhood it was obvious that the young Piccolomini was intelligent, and after some schooling from a local priest he was dispatched

Pope Pius II (Aeneus Sylvius Piccolomini 1458–1464)
Contemporary portrait by Justo di Ghent

to the University of Siena. There he worked hard but plainly played hard too, and soon gained a reputation for being 'a bit of a lad'. Revelling in literature and especially poetry, Enea eventually travelled to Florence, where he studied the Classics for two years and where he gloried in the humanistic circles that were flourishing in the Republic.

In need of employment Piccolomini eventually became secretary to the Bishop of Fermo and travelled with his new master to the Council of Basle, which was held in 1432. There he joined the opposition to the Pope who presently occupied the throne of Peter. This was Eugene IV, a man of little tact who had managed to alienate himself from practically all his Cardinals.

Although maintaining his personal stance against the Pope, Piccolomini changed his employer, opting to work for the richer and more influential Bishop of Freisberg. The Bishop's chief patron was Cardinal Albergati and it was for this man that Piccolomini ultimately came to work. In 1435 the Cardinal sent Piccolomini to Scotland. Even the *Catholic Encyclopaedia* declares this to have been a 'secret mission' and though we have details of Piccolomini's journey we still have no real knowledge of why it was undertaken because the author himself gives more than one version.

Piccolomini was in Scotland for seven months – long enough to father an illegitimate child, and it is highly likely that he had been sent there to sound out the Scottish Cardinals and perhaps also King James I, as to their stance regarding the ever controversial Pope Eugene IV. At the same time Piccolomini himself, in his 'Commentaries', suggests he had been sent to induce the Scottish King to invade England. We know for certain that Piccolomini was at the Scottish Court and so it is inconceivable that he failed to come into contact with Earl William Sinclair. In fact it is a near certainty because we find Earl William communicating directly with Piccolomini at a later date. The nature of the letters seems to give credence to the suggestion that Earl William adopted the illegitimate child fathered by Piccolomini in Scotland and raised it as one of his own.

By this time Piccolomini was already an avid bibliophile. He was a staunch supporter of the humanism that he had encountered in Florence, which was the precursor to the Renaissance, was an avid collector of Classical works and had a very 'liberal' attitude towards Christianity. History relates that it was sometime around the year 1440 that Earl William took it into his head to build a chapel dedicated to St Matthew at Rosslyn and it is highly likely that he discussed his plans with Piccolomini as early as 1435. We have no record of Piccolomini ever coming into contact with Sir Gilbert Haye, who at the time was in France, but the two men had so much in common that it is most unlikely their paths failed to cross at some stage.

Why Piccolomini is important to the story of Rosslyn Chapel is not simply on account of the time he spent in Scotland, except by implication, but rather stems from a later period. Ever an opportunist, Piccolomini was reconciled with Pope Eugene IV in 1445, by which time he had become a high-ranking envoy of Emperor Frederick III. It was in the same year that he took Holy Orders, and after a meteoric rise through various ranks and stations he became Pope Pius II on 19 August 1458.

The new pope clearly intended to make a difference in Rome and across the Christian world, and he did have a good role model. In 1447, whilst Piccolomini had been climbing the ladder towards his own success, Tommaso Parentucelli, another Italian, had been made Pope Nicholas V.

As Pius II Piccolomini would give much to both the Church and the Christian world, but in the estimation of many historians his efforts were based on the model created by Nicholas V. This is not the whole story because Piccolomini, as Nicholas' adviser, had a profound bearing on the role of Nicholas V, and at the very least the two men had similar ideas and inspirations. Nevertheless, from the moment he entered the Vatican Pope Nicholas determined to be a wind of change to an institution he clearly saw as being in need of total modernisation. Nicholas was a scholar, and like both Pius II and Sir Gilbert Haye he was an avid collector of books and a good linguist.

Pope Nicholas immediately encouraged pilgrims to travel to Rome to a greater extent than had ever taken place before. But instead of hoarding away the vast sums of money that came his way as a result he instigated a huge building plan, not only within the Vatican but across the whole of Rome. His care for the poor was legendary and, unlike some of his predecessors, he showed great concern not merely for the souls of his flock but also for their physical well-being. He improved sanitation, built hospitals and saw to it that food was always available for the poor. It is said that no other pope ever spent more on improving the lot of his fellow men, and yet he also found the necessary resources to implement a plan that appears to have been a personal ambition for most of his adult life. It was Pope Nicholas V who first created the Vatican Library.

Not since the days of the great library of Alexandria had such a collection of manuscripts been brought together in one place. Nicholas scoured the recesses of abbeys and churches. He sent emissaries to distant lands, specifically instructed to collect anything of importance in the written word. Where an original manuscript could not be bought, Nicholas used his influence and position to obtain copies and he built a wonderful home for the collection within the walls of the Vatican.

It is clear that Nicholas was not simply a collector of books. This was a genuine library and people came from far and wide to study within its walls. He created what the *Catholic Encyclopaedia* calls 'a vast establishment within the Vatican for translating the Greek Classics' and he welcomed humanists to visit as friends, men who were the sort of free-thinkers who had been viewed with great suspicion by previous popes. During his reign burgeoning Protestantism was delayed in its development, not so much as a result of his laws or military actions but rather because even the zealots saw a Vatican that was changing with the times.

Nicholas also made strenuous attempts to reconcile the different arms of Christianity, making it a personal ambition to reunite the Eastern and Western branches of the Faith. His failure to do so was such a great personal disappointment that it probably contributed to his ill health and early death.

Nicholas reigned as Pope between 1447 and 1455, a comparatively short period, and yet one that was almost certainly crucial to the plans of Earl William Sinclair, far away in Scotland. By the time the Pope died his beloved library contained every scrap of information he could possibly collect, and far from being a collection of books simply dedicated to Christianity his epitaph in vellum contained works on history and world religions from antiquity. Earl William Sinclair had exactly the same aspirations, but instead of dusty tomes that only scholars could comprehend it was clearly William's desire to build the sort of library that could be accessed by anyone – a library in stone. The liberal and outward looking Pope Nicholas V made such a venture tenable, whilst the slightly later reign of Pius II, with its equally humanist slant, offered a continued incentive and gave William a direct conduit to the seat of spiritual power.

It should be remembered that by the time of the investiture of Pius II, according to our estimation of when Rosslyn Chapel was built, the fabric of the building had only been under construction for a mere two years. The appointment of such a man as Piccolomini to the papacy would have been good news indeed to Earl William and Sir Gilbert Haye, with their obviously 'unusual' religious leanings and their vision of the world that mirrored both Nicholas V's and Pius II's own reverence for humanism. It would have been even more useful if, as rumour had it, Earl William had dealt with the new Pope's past indiscretion. It was not unusual for Popes at this period to have illegitimate children, but neither was it something to crow about.

So geared was the new Pope to his humanist approach to life, his liberality of stance and his love of learning and architecture, that had he seen Rosslyn Chapel rising from its mound he would no doubt have applauded both the building and its message. He has gone down in history as being almost unique in his love of the classics, poetry and very unreligious reading matter, making him a true legatee of Nicholas V.

It might seem absurd to question the spiritual leanings of a man who became the head of the Western Christian Church but there is some ambiguity about Pius II's actual religious imperatives. Catholic historians themselves remain puzzled regarding some of his actions. The *Catholic Encyclopaedia* says of him:

> *There have been widely divergent appreciations of the life of Pius II. While his varied talents and superior culture cannot be doubted, the motives of his frequent transfer of allegiance, the causes of the radical transformations which his opinions underwent, the influences exercised over him by the environment in which his lot was cast, are so many factors, the bearing of which can be justly and precisely estimated only with the greatest difficulty.*[16]

It is interesting to note that Piccolomini's transition from a clever but profligate man about town to elder statesman of the Church began not long after his protracted stay in Scotland. Could it be that what he had seen and learned there had a bearing on his subsequent conduct?

Pius II and the Templars

In a strange departure for a man who clearly thought the pen mightier than the sword, almost as soon as he was raised to the papacy, Pope Pius II

16   *The Catholic Encyclopedia*, Editor Robert C Broderick, STL, 1994

took an action that would be staggering if it had worked out as he intended – he appears to have tried to reconstruct the Knights Templar. Whilst the Templars themselves had been censured, disbanded and, where possible, eliminated in the years after 1307, Pope Pius II planned to form an almost identical fighting order which was to be called 'The Knights of Our Lady of Bethlehem'. What makes this departure all the more extraordinary is the fact that one of the monastic orders suppressed to provide money for the new knights was the Order of the Holy Sepulchre. By tradition this order owed its existence to Godfrey de Bouillon, who had led the successful assault on Jerusalem in 1099 and who could have been its first Christian king had he so wished. The Holy Sepulchre is the church built over what is said to have been the burial place of Jesus. It was of great importance to the crusading knights and it is known that many, if not the majority, of the Templar churches were built in its image. (This includes Temple Church, which can still be visited in London.)

The Knights of Our Lady of Bethlehem were to be organised in the same way as the Templars, under a Grand Master, and most tellingly they were to wear white mantles with red crosses – just as the Templars had done. Their proposed base of operation was to be the island of Lemnos in the Aegean Sea, from where it was hoped they could help to stem the tide of Turkish incursions. Unfortunately Lemnos was once more captured by the Turks at precisely the same moment the new order was being formed. As a result the intention, which had been the subject of a solemn and binding Papal Bull, came to nothing.

Is it possible that Pope Pius II was aware that Templarism, or rather the ideas that lay behind it, were far from dead, even by the middle of the 15th century? Since his own religious leanings were more akin to those of the Templars themselves perhaps he was attempting to resurrect the order? Might we also see his sojourn in Scotland as a time when he confronted Ebionite belief at first hand?

The prevailing liberality emanating from Rome during the early phases of the construction of Rosslyn Chapel would have made it relatively easy for Earl William Sinclair to pursue his plans without fear of either interference, or too many questions being asked within the Scottish Church hierarchy. With a tame pope in his pocket and armed with cast-iron explanations for his strange building – in the guise of St Matthew's adventures in Myrna, he could proceed more or less as he wished.

Humanism

Contemporaries heap praise on Earl William as being a man of great generosity and intelligence. There can be little doubt that he espoused the same belief in humanism that prevailed during the reign of Nicholas V and Pius II. Humanism might be described as a new emphasis, evident at the start of the Renaissance, on human culture, education and reason. High on the agenda of humanists were the dignity of man, liberty, equality and brotherhood – the same motivations that would become the war cry of revolutionaries a few centuries later.

The rise of humanism was born out of the fact that access became available to philosophies and religious paths other than those espoused by the established Church. This is in no small part thanks to men such as Nicholas V and Pius II, but in a way they too were simply following the dictates of the age. The existence of the republic of Florence, with its vast wealth, was contributing to a new mind-set across Europe before the reign of the humanist popes. The day of the artist and the artisan was dawning as rich men fought to leave their personal legacy for posterity. The rise of the colossally rich Medici dynasty in Florence coincided with the era of the humanist popes, but whilst later pontiffs sought to prevent the new liberality from getting out of hand, the genie had been let out of the bottle and trying to coax it back proved to be quite impossible. The patronage of Lorenzo de Medici in particular led to the rise of artists such as Leonardo da Vinci and Michelangelo, whilst Cosimo de Medici also built a library to rival that of the Vatican. The shelves of the library in Florence were open to all and its books represented an even more eclectic mixture of subject matter than even the Vatican could boast.

The Vatican had clearly been impressed by what was happening in Florence, the more so because Pope Eugene IV had been forced by circumstance to spend over a decade there between 1434 and 1444.

Meanwhile, Scotland's international outlook and its strong connections with the Continent stood in stark contrast to that of England, and so it is not at all surprising that the seeds of the Renaissance were planted first north of the border.

Assisted by Sir Gilbert Haye, Earl William Sinclair possessed the peculiar and even schismatic religious beliefs, the education, the incentive and the money to create one of the most important and tangible expressions of the changing face of philosophy and religion. It might be fairly suggested that the second half of the 15th century, with its humanist popes and the rise of the Florentine Republic, was the time during which the Renaissance in Europe became a reality and this is exactly the period during which Rosslyn Chapel was constructed. The two facts are not coincidental.

10

The picture book

GREAT LIBRARIES SUCH as those created at the Vatican by Pope Nicholas V and in Florence by the Medici were, themselves, a reflection of the new interest in philosophy and the ancient world. Their very existence mimicked the library of Alexandria and those in Ancient Rome. Ostensibly the new libraries in Italy, just like their earlier counterparts, were available to anyone and the knowledge they contained was intended to speak to humanity as a whole. In practice this could never be the case, either in the ancient or the early Renaissance world. Putting aside the requirement for any given individual to be born of a class that could gain access to such institutions, the first pre-requisite was an ability to read.

Writing and reading

Even by the mid 15th century literacy was the prerogative of the churchman, the scholar and the highborn. Part of the reason for this lay in the fact that any form of education was restricted to those who were expected to fulfil a particular role in life. Someone aspiring to the life of a priest or a monk would need to read and understand the words of the Bible and other religious books. Scholars would of course have to read well, and probably in several languages, especially Latin and Greek. Reading was also becoming necessary for purely social reasons, which is why aristocrats at every level were acquiring the skill for themselves and their sons. Courtly behaviour and manners began to require a familiarity with songs, poems and stories that inferred greater status on those who studied and understood them. Reading was also becoming necessary to the merchant, the lawyer, the banker, the shipper and to a host of others whose skills contributed to the efficient running of an increasingly complex society.

Nevertheless the vast majority of individuals in Medieval Europe remained blissfully ignorant as far as the written word was concerned. This was not merely a reflection of the feudal notion that 'everyone should know and keep his place' because even if some monarch had suddenly and inexplicably declared that all his subjects, no matter how base, should learn to read, there would not have been enough books to go round. It is a fact that until the mid 15th century – exactly contemporary with the building of Rosslyn Chapel, every single word committed to any sort of document had to be written by hand.

After the decline of the Roman Empire and the eventual arrival of Christianity to Western Europe the only texts that existed were religious in nature. These were bibles, prayer books, stories of the lives of saints or other Christian tracts. Such works were meticulously copied by monks in the scriptoriums of their abbeys and by a few secular copyists working for the upper aristocracy and royalty. This was the case in Rosslyn where Sir Gilbert Haye set up his scriptorium in Rosslyn Castle in 1456, the remnants of which can still be seen today.

Copying manuscripts was a laborious job and the need for religious books constantly outstripped the ability of the literate to produce them. The situation was made even worse during the time of the Black Death in the 14th century. The plague was not mindful of class or station and monasteries suffered more than most institutions, not because a disproportionate number of brothers succumbed to the pestilence but because after the plague society could not afford to send its depleted ranks of sons to the abbey when there were acres to plough, and crops to be harvested.

The law of supply and demand was, in this respect at least, as operative in feudal Europe as it is today, and so books of any sort were prohibitively expensive. They were owned only by the Church and by those with large amounts of surplus money, and were so precious that when they were sometimes put on display, they were retained with stout chains in order to prevent theft.

As far as the orthodox Church was concerned this inability on the part of the masses to read or write was no problem. In fact it was actually a boon because it put priests very much in the driving seat. The word of God was written in Scripture and in any given parish it was a safe bet that just about the only man who could read from the scriptures was the local priest. This put him in the same position of strength as the astronomer/priests of ancient times who could predict eclipses of the sun – it gave them real power and status. Even when printing presses were invented the Church fought long and hard to prevent Bibles in particular from reaching worshipers directly, because in that direction lay a loss of mystique and a degradation of authority.

All the same it was important for Christian believers, no matter how lowly their status, to understand the major themes of their religion. This was all the more necessary since church services were held in Latin, a language spoken by very few outside of the church and the law.

So prior to the Reformation the average parish church or cathedral across most of Europe was a riot of colour. Walls were painted with scenes from the life of Jesus, Old Testament stories and tales from the Anti-Nicene Fathers. Since there were no pews or seats in most churches, the priest could perambulate about the body of his church, followed by his congregation, pointing to the various pictures, whilst explaining the stories they represented. Likewise there were carvings in wood and stone, statues of Biblical characters, reliquaries that held the relics of saints, together with framed paintings and luxurious tapestries, all of which were designed to inform the illiterate and to spread the message of the Gospels. The Church year trundled on from Christmas to Easter and back to Christmas. The rites of Christian passage were played out in the lives of generations of ordinary people who were baptised, married and buried, often in the same parish church where their fathers and grandfathers had worshiped.

Printing

All of this came to a fairly abrupt end with the invention of the printing press. Although printing with wooden blocks had been practised for years in China, it took the ingenuity of Johann Gutenburg, a man born into a family of metal workers and minters in Mainz, to invent the system of printing that would change the world.

Gutenburg, in addition to being proficient at gem polishing and metal engraving, was an inventor. Little is known about the circumstances that led up to his creation of moveable type but we do know that by 1453 he was producing a '42 line bible'. Sadly Johann did not prosper much from his invention, but others were quick to see its potential. The process of laying down type made from metal to create text, and then to print it onto vellum, and eventually paper, raced around Europe with lightning speed. By 1472 an Englishman by the name of William Caxton, a powerful mercer and wool merchant from Kent, had set up a printing press in Bruges and had created the first printed book ever to appear in the English language. This was *Recuyell of the Historyes of Troye,* and was followed by many others once Caxton returned to England and created his press in London in 1476.

Ultimately the art of printing would make books available to all, and not simply the religious tracts that had been penned for centuries in the monasteries. Soon there were stories, political treaties, pamphlets and

Johann Gutenburg (1400–1468) Inventor of the first printing press

almanacs. Suddenly there was a greater incentive for anyone, no matter how lowly, to become literate, and though both Church and State tried hard to hold back the flood tide, it was to no avail.

The same changing world that led to the creation of moveable type printing was fully in operation as Rosslyn Chapel was being constructed. This makes the chapel a building created 'right on the edge', at a time when new ideas were taking Europe by storm but still during a period when symbolism was supremely important to a largely illiterate populace. This, probably above all other considerations, is what sets Rosslyn Chapel apart and is the chief reason why it represents one of the undeniable treasures of history.

The forces within society that were unleashed by printing and the availability of the printed word were unstoppable. Access to knowledge made ordinary people aware that they were being hoodwinked by Rome. Dissident priests, such as Martin Luther (1483-1546), who would formerly have been silenced and burned as heretics, committed their accusations about the Church to writing. The prerogative was no longer with the parish priest and the view of the world from grass roots level quickly began to change. It took only one member of the average society – perhaps

Martin Luther (1483–1546), leading protagonist of the Reformation

an educated shopkeeper, to learn the skill of reading and to acquire a few seditious pamphlets in order to change the view of his peers and to enlighten them as to the duplicity of Rome and its corrupt spiritual rulers.

Without the invention of printing the religious reformations that began in Germany early in the 16th century and then shot round Western Europe like a rocket could never have taken place. But all of this was a generation or two away from Earl William Sinclair and Sir Gilbert Haye as they surveyed the hills to the east of Rosslyn in order to ensure the correct orientation of their new creation.

Writing in stone

We have shown that Earl William and Gilbert Haye were more than familiar with the concepts of humanism that were even being espoused within the Vatican itself as they began to build the village that would house those who would complete the chapel. William's tremendous generosity to his workers bears testimony to the importance he placed upon these values. Not only did he set up a new village for them, to replace the old medieval settlement that was situated opposite the castle on the other side of the River Esk in Rosslyn Glen (part of the bridge linking the old village with the castle still exists), Earl William also paid them handsomely for their efforts. Surviving records bear testimony to the fact that Master craftsmen were paid £40 per year and other craftsmen including stonemasons received £10 annually. These were large sums at the time.

With what were obviously 'peculiar' religious beliefs and practices, most likely inherited from lineal sources that could be traced back for countless generations, Sinclair and Haye looked towards a world in which rank, station and brute force would not be half so important as philosophy and intention. Though they could hardly guess at what would take place in the centuries after their deaths, they clearly saw that their time had come.

Utilising the same techniques that had been employed by the Church for centuries, Sinclair and Haye determined to construct a building that would represent, in a comparatively small space, the accumulated knowledge that might be found in a large library of books, although edited into a carved stone, cartoon picture form, that could be understood by all, foreigner, scribe or unlettered peasant. As an immediate indication that here was something very special, the building style itself would be a compendium of architectural techniques, a kind of visual builder's manual or handbook.

Sinclair and Haye may have been disposed towards humanism and philosophy but there is no doubt that both had a deep and abiding belief in God. It was nowhere near enough to create the finest masterpieces in stone that were possible within the building or even outside at the lower levels. On the roof, each and every pinnacle had to be slightly different than its neighbours. Heralding that all sentient beings were unique in the eyes of God, these cosmetic differences would be absolutely invisible from the ground but the Almighty would see them and know this to be a very special place – the very best that humanity could create.

Paradise

From first to last the interior of Rosslyn Chapel was intended to be a 'Paradise'. Most of the carvings on the exterior of the building are of ordinary medieval people as well as superb grotesques. There are monsters for water spouts, hideous gargoyle faces that peer out from between the windows and above ledges, impossible beasts, gryphons and creatures of the dark forest –

Even the external waterspouts of Rosslyn Chapel are masterpieces of the carver's art

though even here Sinclair and Haye could not avoid hinting at a world far beyond Scotland. On the south wall there is an exquisite carving of a monkey (doubtless a creature that was rarely if ever seen in 15th century Scotland) and another equally fascinating carving of a camel with two humps. This makes it a camel of the Bactrian sort. At the time Rosslyn Chapel was built Bactrian camels were only to be found in Turkmenia, Persia, Mongolia and China. They were to be seen plodding in caravans along the Silk Road and the presence of this representation at Rosslyn is no doubt a legacy of Gilbert Haye's visit to far off Cathay.

If you have visited Rosslyn Chapel, or even seen some of the exquisite photographs that have been taken of its interior, dismiss the muted tones of the stone but keep the images in your mind. Now close your eyes and in your imagination paint all areas of the chapel with bright and vibrant colours. Make the leaves and vines various hues of green, complimented

The pinnacle on the roof of the Chapel that is also a carefully created beehive

The famous Veil of Veronica carving

by red and white roses. See in your mind's eye those elusive Green Men, now picked out at boss ends and amongst the shrubbery in wonderful russets with splashes of sienna and ochre. Give the angels good flesh tones and dress them in costumes of orange, purple and glittering gold. Clothe the musicians, the dancers and the peasants in plaids and colourful shawls. Imagine the roof alive with silver stars set in a deep blue firmament – with multi-coloured flowers and fleur-de-lis.

From all corners vibrant faces peer out at you, adorned with flaxen or nut-brown tresses, the luxuriant beards of the patriarchs streaked with silver and grey and their eyes sparkling with life. In the main body of the chapel are representations from the New Testament. At the top of one column Jesus is forced to kneel before Pontius Pilate, whilst elsewhere St Veronica stoops to wipe his face with that now famous veil. The effect would be overwhelming, electrifying and to people who saw little colour in their day-to-day lives except that created by nature, utterly awe-inspiring. In this age of naked stonework we forget that the stone-carver's art, no matter how elevated, was not the end product, which was left to the artist with his sable brushes and rich pigments.

In addition to the carvings there were once also statues in the chapel, standing in niches around the walls. John had long suspected that the twelve empty niches in the main body of the chapel must have once housed statues of the twelve Apostles, the original disciples of Jesus. Proof came for us with the discovery of a book entitled *Stories of Rosslyn Castle*, by an author called Johnstone, published in 1822. The book is a fascinating collection of tales, inspired by papers found in a vault in Rosslyn Castle.

One of these stories relates specifically to the statues within Rosslyn Chapel. Johnstone tells a story that took place in the reign

Portrait of Mary Queen of Scots (1542–1587), whose fondness for Rosslyn Chapel nearly led to its destruction

of Mary Queen of Scots, and whilst she was actually present in Scotland as an adult (1561-1568). Mary was a staunch Catholic but she ruled a divided realm. The forces of Protestantism, headed by John Knox, were gaining the ascendancy in Scottish religion, though Mary continued to practice her own faith. Knox preached against "idolatry" with the greatest fervour, and with the result that his followers, whom he calls the "rascal multitude" began the "purging and cleansing" of churches and the gradual destruction of monasteries. John Knox mentioned in one of his sermons in Edinburgh that Mary, when resident at Craigmillar Castle, loved to take mass at Rosslyn Chapel and the small chapel of Woodhouselee not far from Rosslyn. This was enough for the mob.

Inflamed by this fact and stirred up by other supporters of Knox, the angry mob assembled and marched to Rosslyn, determined to destroy those chapels where Mary had continued her Catholic devotions. Arriving at Rosslyn to cries of 'Smash the Apostles' the vandals entered the chapel and tore down the twelve statues from their niches. They fell to the floor below and were smashed into thousands of pieces. All the figures in the niches seem to have suffered the same fate, simply because they were the easiest of the carvings to destroy. Fortunately a quick-witted local farmer by the name of Thomas Cochrane was also in the vicinity. With great presence of mind he turned the attention of the Edinburgh mob away from the chapel and towards the large amounts of alcohol to be found in the nearby castle. He led the crowd to the castle where they broke into the store, stole the alcohol and dispersed with their booty before the forces of law and order arrived. If the statues in question were of the same quality as the other carvings, inside and outside the chapel, their loss is lamentable, but how much worse things might have been but for the resourceful Cochrane.

The meaning

So how would a typical worshipper of the 15th century have viewed Rosslyn Chapel? It is obvious that the colourful carvings, as in any church of the period, were meant to be an aid to learning. Most members of the congregation would have rarely, if ever, wandered any further east than the main body of the building, generally referred to as the Choir. It is here that are to be found images that almost exclusively relate to the New Testament of the Bible. This was the part of the Christian story that would have been most familiar to the average worshiper of the period. Using the carvings in this part of the chapel the resident priest could explain about Jesus' life and mission, his death and the subsequent spread of his teachings via the Apostles.

Further towards the east we begin to encounter images that are Old Testament in theme. Here are carvings of the patriarchs, probably including Moses, a figure who is shown with horns – a strange departure to the modern observer but one that is mirrored in other ecclesiastical buildings of the period. The same horns or the horn-like shapes seen in the hair of several of the angels in Rosslyn are said to denote their importance, that they were angels with whom God was personally familiar.

Other carvings may represent Old Testament prophets such as Ezekiel or Elijah but the main themes around the division between the Choir and the Retro-Choir mostly seem to be centred on the story of the building of Solomon's Temple, its destruction

Many observers claim this to be a representation of King Darius of Old Testament and Jerusalem Chapel fame

and the ultimate creation of the Second Temple in Jerusalem. It is here at the pillar tops that we find the musicians and where there is also an exquisite carving that could easily represent Darius, the Persian King who allowed the Hebrews to return to Jerusalem after their long captivity.

Of course we must not forget the story of St Matthew because, after all, the whole chapel is dedicated to him. At various times throughout the year his story would be told to the assembled congregation and particularly on 21 September, his feast day. The wonderful pillar to the south east would be explained in terms of this story as representative of St Matthew's staff and the wonderful Tree of Life that sprang from it. The priest would point out the luxuriant foliage around the chapel; all emanating from this one pillar and remind his attentive flock about the paradise created in Myrna, no doubt drawing in stories of the Garden of Eden prior to the Fall of Man. The deeper meanings of this pillar, its two neighbours and the naturalistic elements of the chapel would remain completely unknown to the vast majority of worshipers – as indeed they remain generally unknown today.

Little by little, as their lives ran on from season to season, the ordinary people of Rosslyn would become conversant with the themes of the Christian story, almost in a seasonal journey, and the deeper significance of the chapel and its carvings would remain a mystery. However, in the case of those who could be trusted with the secrets, and especially Sinclair family members, the carvings and the chapel itself could impart a very much deeper message. In a secular sense "the chapel amidst the woods", could represent 'the Green Chapel' from *Sir Gawain and the Green Knight*, a tale that was phenomenally popular at the time, with its humanistic message of modesty, honesty and chivalry. Other secular stories such as *Alexander's Journey to Paradise* are played out amidst the vines and foliage – a story that was also of the most tremendous importance in 15th century Europe. Its tales of a semi-mythological Alexander the Great pointed at important philosophical truths, based around the espoused wisdom of the Greek philosopher Aristotle, who had been Alexander's teacher.

The teaching of Aristotle was of supreme significance to the rising humanism of the period. It was taken on board by the revolutionary Christian thinker St Thomas Aquinas (1225-1274) who himself had been influenced by the earlier Jewish philosopher Maimonides (1135-1204). Aristotle had taught that knowledge of the world could only be gained via the senses. He was a shrewd observer and his immensely influential teaching set the scene for the empirical scientific model that would become so important to post-Reformation Europe.

In addition Aristotle was thought to be responsible for a book called *The Secretum Secretorum*, a work that Sir Gilbert Haye had personally translated. The alternative title of *Secretum Secretorum* (literally "Secret of Secrets") is 'The Book of the Science of Government, on the Good Ordering of Statecraft'. In reality it is most likely of Arabic origin from a work entitled 'Kitab sirr al-asrar', though its ultimate origins are unknown. The *Secretum Secretorum* represents a letter, supposedly sent by Aristotle to his former student Alexander, and details specific information on living a successful, pious and just life. It was a philosophical guidebook on how a Prince or a King should treat his subjects, again bringing out the essence of humanism, and the importance of respecting each unique, individual person irrespective of their station in life.

To the truly initiated Rosslyn Chapel took on a unique form. St Matthew's staff or pillar, with its two companions, representing the three trunks of the Kabalistic Tree of Life and the paradise emanating from them, was nothing more or less than a representation of the New Jerusalem.

This was a New Jerusalem that rejected the institutionalised church, and promoted the ideal that mankind did not need an earthly organisation to speak to God, that each individual had the ability and the right of access, through the strength of their own faith. To the initiated St Matthew's pillar was also the natural conduit between Heaven and Earth, which embodies both the Shekinah and her male aspect, the Metatron. This explains the great profusion of angel carvings within the chapel. They are the attendants of the Shekinah and the Metatron, populating the symbolic, heavenly paradise on Earth that Rosslyn Chapel represents.

The building

The true significance of the chapel to the initiated lay not only in its rich carvings and their true meaning, but also in the building as a whole. The chapel was specifically built to have a strong cosmological significance – mirroring the astronomical knowledge of the builders of Solomon's

Ogive or Gothic Arch built around a Pentacle¹

---

1   Original idea from *The Mysteries of Chartres Cathedral* by Louis Charpentier, AB Academic Publishers, London, 1997

Temple. Astronomical understanding was further emphasised by the use of a barrel-vaulted roof, which echoes the arch of heaven observable above our heads. There can be no doubt about this intention because the western end of the chapel roof is a mass of stars, and also contains a sun, moon and other symbols that may represent planets.

The secrets that lay within the geometry used to build the chapel are complex, but since the building is basically Gothic in design, like all Gothic structures it is inspired by proportions that had been considered sacred for centuries. The rounded and pointed arches upon which much of the building depends for its strength as well as its beauty have a geometric significance of their own. The Gothic arch, or ogive, may have its origins in Islamic architecture. It is immensely strong but fiendishly difficult to create. However, there is one sure-fire way to obtain the correct proportions and that is by creating the arch around a pentacle or five-pointed star. (See Chapter 11)

The five-pointed star or pentacle was of tremendous importance to ancient religion, as well as Christianity, and would ultimately take a central role in Freemasonry. Part of the significance of the arch built around the pentacle lays in its recognition of the human proportions of the pentacle shape. This recognition that the human body itself, complete with head, arms and legs fits well

The human body inside a pentacle. (Attributed to Cornelius Agrippa)

inside the upright pentacle was part of an early understanding regarding that magical proportion known as the golden mean and the part it plays in the physics of the natural world. Such knowledge, even by the 15th century, was not something to crow about, especially in ecclesiastical circles.

The music?

Only with time and many visits to the chapel does it begin to dawn on the observer just how much physical work went into this masterpiece. Unlike any other Gothic structure we have ever seen, each of the arches in the Retro Choir carry intricately carved cubes of stone along their length – 213 of them in total, each with a unique pattern etched onto its lower side. It has been suggested that within these cubes lies a coded message that could be musical in nature. One of the theories presently being investigated is that the patterns represent shapes formed in sand sprinkled on brass or copper plates. When the plate is excited by a bow, the sand dances and

The top of the Journeyman Pillar showing cubes in place along arches
Inset: Pattern on one of the Rosslyn cubes. (Courtesy of Scotsman Newspaper)

forms similar patterns to those shown on the cubes. These are known as Chladni patterns.

Warwick Edwards from Glasgow University Music Department considers that the lines could represent a 15th century way of representing musical notes. He suggests that at the time no universal form of musical notation existed and he is far from being alone in his opinions. Edinburgh composer Stuart Mitchell thinks he has cracked the musical code. Perhaps strangely he announced his success in the same week that Tom Hanks and the Hollywood circus were filming at Rosslyn. His father, Thomas Mitchell, is said to have spent 20 years working on the possibilities, leaving Stuart to orchestrate the results for a piece of music he calls *The Rosslyn Motet*.[17]

Mitchell suggests that if the notes shown on the cubes are played repeatedly within the building, they will unlock a chamber in which the treasure of Rosslyn may be found, and with this statement yet another story is added to the plethora of tales regarding the chapel, that in time become legends in their own right. Mark Naples, another knowledgeable young scholar who has spent several years researching the cubes, repudiates Mitchell's hypothesis, believing that Mitchell has miscounted the cubes.

Carvings of musicians, one group of whom can be seen just above the capitol of the Master's Pillar, may be a clue to the musical notation indicated by the cubes but they are just as likely to relate to the celebrations for the Feast of Tabernacles, as demonstrated by a passage from the Book of Samuel in the Old Testament of the Bible.

'After that thou shalt come to the hill of God, where is the garrison of the Philistines: and it shall come to pass, when thou art come thither to the city, that thou shalt meet a company of prophets coming down from the high place with a psaltery, and a tabret, and a pipe, and a harp, before them; and they shall prophesy.' Samuel Chapter 10 V5.

The musicians are even more likely to refer to a passage in the 2nd Book of Chronicles that tells of an event that took place at the time of the dedication of Solomon's Temple. The Ark of the Covenant had been placed in the Holy of Holies for the first time and when the assembled musicians began to play those officiating were overcome by a mysterious cloud that

---

17 Article by Leighton Bruce, Scotsman Newspaper, 27 April 2006

The musicians on the Master's Pillar, Rosslyn Chapel

was said to be the Glory of God – a manifestation of the Shekinah. This event took place on the first day of the month of Tishri, the day of the Jewish New Year in September, a period that was synonymous with St Matthew's Day and the Autumn Equinox.

It came even to pass, as the trumpeters and singers were as one, to make one sound to be heard in praising and thanking the LORD; and when they lifted up their voice with the trumpets and cymbals and instruments of music, and praised the LORD, saying, For he is good; for his mercy endureth for ever: that then the house was filled with a cloud, even the house of the LORD;

So that the priests could not stand to minister by reason of the cloud: for the glory of the LORD had filled the house of God. 2 Chronicles Chapter 5 Verse 13.

There is yet another possible explanation for the presence of the musicians. In the 1st Book of Esdras the story is told of Zerubbabel returning from captivity in Babylon in order to rebuild and found the second Temple in Jerusalem. As the freed captives arrived at this most important place there was great rejoicing. Esdras tells us:

And the priests stood arrayed in their vestments with musical instruments and trumpets; and the Levites the sons of Asaph had cymbals. 1 Esdras Chapter 5 Verse 59.

The plants

If the musicians can be dealt with by reference to the Old Testament, some of the plants carved around the chapel walls are much more difficult to explain. This is particularly true of the examples of 'maize', which has been a great puzzle to those trying to interpret Rosslyn's carvings.

Ears of maize carved into the stonework of Rosslyn Chapel

Whilst many of the plants depicted in the carvings are clearly of indigenous species the same cannot be said to be the case with regard to maize. There can be no doubt that this is what the stone-carvers intended to represent and there is no Western European species that looks remotely like maize (or Indian Corn, as it is sometimes called).

The plant depicted in these carvings, more properly called 'Zea mays' is a plant of the Americas. The type of maize grown today could never been found in the wild because it has been cultivated and gradually changed by man, probably for as much as 7,000 years. Maize production most likely began in Mexico but by 1,000 years ago cultivation had spread up into the body of North America, and at the time of the arrival of the first Europeans it was the staple food source of the Indians living in what is now called New England.

As far as the history books are concerned Europeans did not encounter maize until their arrival in Central America with the expedition of Hernando Cortez, who defeated the Aztecs and subjugated their empire around 1519. This was a good forty years after Rosslyn Chapel was completed and the position of the maize plants carved into the chapel indicates that they have been in place all along. Historians may pour scorn upon the theory that William's grandfather, Prince Henry Sinclair, had visited America, or at the very least had financed expeditions across the Atlantic, but they fail to address the fact that a specifically American plant was accurately depicted in Rosslyn before Christopher Columbus had been given command of so much as a rowing boat. There seems no credible explanation for its presence unless someone associated with the building of the chapel had seen the plant at firsthand.

The famous aloe cactus depicted in the chapel may be easier to explain. Aloes grew in Morocco and along the African coast and aloes had been imported to Europe and used as curative balm long before Rosslyn was built. If the inspiration for the aloes depicted within Rosslyn Chapel had actually come from the Americas, its existence must have been reported by travellers who had sailed very far down the eastern seaboard, almost to Mexico.

Layer on layer the library in stone divulges its secrets. Despite the number of years we have been visiting the chapel we do not pretend to be party to all its messages. Rosslyn Chapel does speak to us but it isn't always easy to understand what is being said and several lifetimes would probably not be enough to explore every possibility in full.

11

The light box

$\mathbf{W}$E WERE NOT particularly surprised when we came across a persistent rumour regarding one of the windows of Rosslyn Chapel. Legend has it that on a particular day each year (a day which was unspecified in the rumour) such was the position of the window (also unspecified) and the rising sun that light would stream in and illuminate the niche of a now missing statue. Since we could not tie the rumour down to a specific window or a particular date on the calendar, for years we dismissed the assertion as being little more than a fairy tale, on a par with the iridescent blue door some 'sensitives' are supposed to see in the north east corner of the chapel or the mysterious lights that are said to glow within the chapel, predicting the imminent death of a Sinclair family member.

In all probability, we reasoned, some mix-up had arisen regarding Rosslyn Chapel. Perhaps people were confusing it with the equally popular and enigmatic Chartres Cathedral, in France, where such a window does exist and where a beam of light streaming through a plain pane of glass illuminates a specific part of the Cathedral on mid summer day. Something similar takes place in the equally mysterious Church of St Sulpice in Paris, where the beam of light illuminates a metal channel set into the floor of the knave, highlighting France's prime meridian, which used to run through the church. In the absence of any obviously plain piece of glass in any of the windows of Rosslyn Chapel and with no definite story on which to pin our research, for years we ignored the story.

Matters came to a head in the late spring of 2006. We had come into possession of a number of early photographs dating back to the 1840s, and these fascinating sepia prints showed us just how bad the state of repair of the chapel had become by the early 19th century. Many windows were smashed or missing altogether and the building was as good as open to the elements.

Many of John's relatives still live in and around Rosslyn and he happened to show some of the old photographs to his mother's cousin. They were remarking to each other that the large east window of the chapel had been completely recreated during the Victorian restorations. The crenulated stonework of the upper part of the window and in fact the whole rose window itself, was absent in the earlier design, and at the time of the 1830 photographs all the glass within the east window had been smashed.

John's cousin, Nancy, looked with interest at the old photographs and remarking particularly about the east window she made the casual comment, "I see the small hole for the light to pass through on St Matthew's Day was already there on the old east window."

John was fascinated and asked Nancy what she meant. She explained that she remembered that as a child and a young woman she had been present in the chapel very early on St Matthew's Day to see sunlight stream in through an aperture at the top of the east window. All of this had taken place many years ago and she could not remember at what exact time of day the sunlight had broken into the chapel or where it had fallen within the building when it did.

The story galvanised John into action. Gathering together his equipment, and in particular the longest telephoto lens he possessed, he left the chapel, where he had been talking to Nancy, and went to a position from which he had a good view of the east window. Focussing on the small, dark spot in the very point of the window's arch he took a movie clip, zooming in as much as was possible. The result was stunning. Not only was there a clear, five-sided hole in the masonry, but it was plain to see from a close-up image that the hole was lined with some sort of metal (see colour section).

John now returned to the chapel interior and took pictures of the arch above the window from the inside of the building. The hole was less evident here, mainly because the light was dimmer, but it was still plain to see. We could not tell whether or not the inside hole occupied a slightly lower position relative to the point of the arch. As a result it was impossible at first to tell whether the hole through the masonry was angled downwards, indicating that a beam of light passing through it would not simply traverse the chapel at roof level, but rather cascade down somewhere into the body of the chapel itself.

Relative to the size of the wall and the East Window it was obvious that the hole was not large, perhaps seven or eight inches across and from the ground it simply looks like part of the ornamentation of the stone window frame. John passed the information he had gained to Alan, who began looking at the hole from an astronomical point of view and we discussed this obviously deliberately created 'light box' for some days.

The light box occupies a position in the very centre of the east end of the building. (The reader will recall that the chapel is built on a true east/west alignment.) Only under very specific circumstances could

The east window of Rosslyn Chapel

light from the rising sun penetrate the light box and shine through into the chapel. This could only happen when the sun was exactly due east of the chapel just after dawn. It was immediately obvious that such a set of circumstances only makes itself available twice in each year. As we have already observed, the sun occupies different points of the eastern horizon at dawn throughout the changing year. Only during the two equinoxes, spring and autumn, (March and September) does the sun rise due east, cross the sky to the south before arcing north and then setting due west. It was only on these two days each year that the sun would occupy a position on the horizon that would allow its light to pass through the light box and into the chapel. And the Autumn Equinox occurs on 21 September, which is of course St Matthew's Day.

A great deal of thought and planning had gone into the positioning of the light box in terms of its placement on the east wall of the chapel. This could be no accident – it was intended to create a particular effect at a very specific time of year. But the rediscovery of the light box raised a number of questions.

It was obvious from the moment we saw John's footage that the light box was lined with sheet metal. What was especially surprising about the metal is that it reflects sunlight extremely well. This might not seem especially odd until one realises just how long the light box has been in place. Most metal tarnishes and had the lining been any type of iron or steel, it would surely be badly corroded since it is not protected from the weather in any way. Lead would have turned black in a matter of years, copper would have gone green and even silver would have eventually turned black. At the time the lining of the light box was put in place there was only one type of metal available that would have remained bright despite the passing of the years and the constant bombardment of the weather and that would have been gold.

Another important question was whether or not the light box had existed before the chapel window was recreated in the 1870s. Photographs of the chapel from the 1840s, though showing the East Window, were not taken close enough to the building to allow a good view of the place where the light box would have been. But of course there is a further consideration. The East Window could not have been totally recreated in Victorian times, as we know it was, without those responsible becoming aware of the light box and its obvious purpose, assuming of course that it existed in the original window. The inevitable conclusions must be:

- that the light box was left alone during the recreation of the window,
- that it was recreated at that time,
- or that it was actually created for the first time in the 1860s.

The pentagon

We now turned our attention to the shape of the light box. It forms a five-sided figure, in other words a pentagon, like the one below.

Without very accurate measurements being taken, which bearing in mind the position of the light box is impossible at present, it is difficult to tell whether the light box represents a regular pentagon, in other words whether all its angles and sides are the same, but the fact that it is a pentagon at all could turn out to be very important.

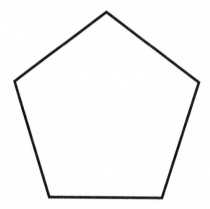

The pentagon has been a significant figure for many centuries. It has some interesting properties and enshrines what has been known from Ancient Greek times as the 'golden mean', otherwise known as the 'golden section'. The golden section refers to a measurement that appears regularly in nature. It is best demonstrated by way of the diagram below.

The top line has been split into line A and line B. If the length of the dotted line B has a relationship to the size of line A that is the same as the relationship of line A to line C, this is a golden section.

This might sound rather complicated but it is one of the fundamental building blocks of nature and appears all over the universe, from the

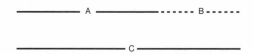

smallest snail shell to the greatest spiral galaxy. The golden section actually represents a ratio, which is 1.618 : 1 and this ratio is enshrined in a regular pentagon. In Ancient Greek times this relationship was already understood and was incorporated into the design of many Greek temples.

If we take our pentagon and, as in the example below, and draw within it a five-pointed star, known as a 'pentagram' or a 'pentacle', it can be observed that the line ABC conforms to the golden section in that the length of BC is to AB what AB is to AC. The same is true of the line ADE and of course all other lines in the construction.

This is partly what has made the pentagon and the pentagram so important and magical for so many centuries. Examples of the pentacle created from the pentagon have come down to us from Ancient Sumer and Babylon, Egypt, Greece and countless other cultures.

Over the last couple of centuries the pentacle has attracted a good deal

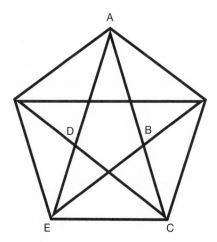

of attention because it has become fixed in the mind of many individuals as some sort of magical symbol, with demonic or satanic overtones. In fact nothing could be further from the truth because the pentacle was originally widely used as a symbol within Christianity itself and represented the five wounds of Christ. In addition it has close associations with the shape of the common dog rose, which also has a special place in Christianity[18]. Modern witchcraft does, like many other beliefs over the years, make much of the pentacle but assertions that the pentacle has something to do with the Devil only really surfaced in the 19th century, and these were generally directed at the importance of the device to Freemasonry. These days the internet especially is filled with assertions that the pentacle has demonic overtones but its use in the West most definitely stems from its Judaeo/Christian associations. To the Jews it represented a device known as the 'Seal of Solomon', though these days the name Seal of Solomon is usually ascribed to a six-pointed star, which also has an importance in Judaism.

Probably because of the now generally accepted 'magical' status of the pentacle, Freemasonry has recently tried to divorce itself from the symbol. However it was once widely used in the Craft in the form of a lamp that shone at the east end of the Masonic Temple, specifically when a candidate was raised to the Third Degree. Regalia from historical Masonic America regularly carries examples of the pentacle, and this includes the Masonic Apron worn by President George Washington when he officiated at the laying of the cornerstone for the Capitol building in Washington DC on 19 September 1793. No matter how unfortunate the public perception may be with regard to the pentacle, Freemasonry cannot deny that it was a symbol that the Craft once used regularly and held in reverence. As a five-pointed star, and therefore without its visible construction lines, the pentacle is still used as the Masonic symbol known as the 'Blazing Star' and is found on the US flag and on the Great Seal of the United States. But it should be noted that when the pentacle does carry its construction lines, a second, but this time inverted pentagon appears at its centre. In other words you can't have one without the other.

The pentacle and therefore the pentagon from which it originates also have strong cosmological associations. This is because of the strange relationship between the orbital period of the Earth and the observed orbital period of the planet Venus (synodic period). As we mentioned in Chapter 7, whilst the Earth takes 365.25 days to orbit the sun, when seen from Earth Venus appears to take 584 days. There is a close correlation between the two in that eight Earth years are equivalent to five cycles of Venus, to within a couple of days. This is very close to being a true

---

18 *The Goddess, the Grail and the Lodge*, Alan Butler, O Books, 2004

golden section relationship because if we divide 584 by 365 we arrive at 1.6, whereas the true golden section ratio is 1.618:1. In addition, during an eight-year period, during which time Venus completes five full cycles, it can be seen that it scribes a theoretical five-pointed star or pentacle across the heavens. Its finishing point after five full cycles will always be close to that from which it started in terms of its position within the zodiac.

When one considers that the light box in Rosslyn Chapel could have been any shape, it is rather odd that the pentagon was the preferred shape, particularly considering the Freemasonic and Venus overtones. Bearing these possible connections in mind we have to ask ourselves whether or not the light box was created 'only' to allow sunlight to pass through into the chapel on the Autumn and Spring equinoxes?

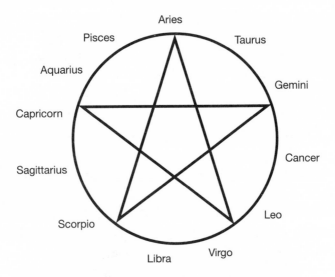

The five pointed star created by Venus as it passes through the heavens (as seen from Earth) Any event of Venus, such as the planet appearing at maximum elongation, will recreate itself four more times in different parts of the zodiac before returning after eight years to its starting point

Venus

First of all we tried to establish whether it would be possible to view the all-important Shekinah through the Rosslyn light box. It did not take long to establish the answer. The light box is like a telescope pointed at a particular place, which is fixed by the position of the entire chapel. In other words it points relentlessly and perpetually at the eastern horizon. This is where the conjunction of Mercury and Venus would be seen if it occurred on either the Spring or the Autumn Equinox. The Shekinah could therefore cast its light into the light box.

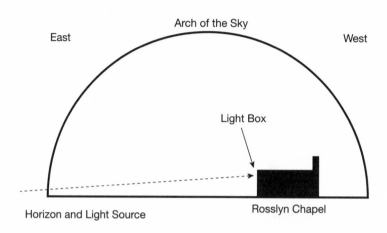

The light from any object that penetrates the light box at Rosslyn Chapel has to be positioned immediately above the eastern horizon

It seems unlikely that the light box was created specifically with the Shekinah in mind, since the time periods between its appearances in the light box would be in the order of many hundreds of years. And though we cannot rule out this possibility, a far more likely scenario is that the light box was built not simply to allow sunlight to pass through it each 21 March and 21 September but also with the planet Venus in mind. The pentagonal shape of the light box may indeed be offering us a clue that this is the case.

Since Venus appears regularly as a morning star, its appearances in the light box would be far more frequent than that of the Shekinah. However, although Venus could shine into the light box on either 21 September or 21 March if the planet was close to the sun as a morning star, it would also be ideally placed to do so at other times.

Any light source entering the light box must be positioned just above the horizon and in a due east position. When Venus appears as a morning star and rises well ahead of the sun, it achieves this objective fairly

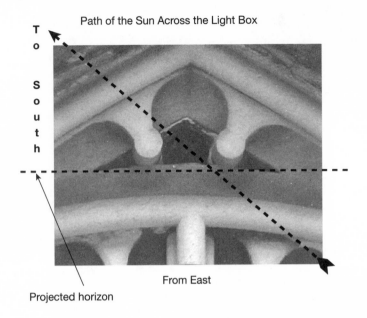

Path of the Sun Across the Light Box

To

South

Projected horizon

From East

frequently. As an example, in the year 2007, assuming that the sky is clear of cloud, the sun will shine into the Rosslyn light box at just after 6am on 21 September. However, although Venus will be a morning star at this time, it will be rising well ahead of the sun and the point at which it breaks the horizon will be significantly north of east. It is not until around 3am on the morning of the following 10 November that Venus will rise exactly due east and so therefore shine into the light box. The closer Venus is to the sun within the zodiac as a morning star, the nearer to 21 March and 21 September will be its appearances in the light box. Venus will shine into the light box on at least one day in most years, though there are years in which it does not and others when the phenomenon happens twice.

Discovering those occasions on which Venus will cast her light into the light box is easy these days, utilising accurate planetary tables and sophisticated electronic planetariums. This was certainly not the case in the 15th century and the only entirely accurate way to make such judgements then would have been by a mixture of mathematics and manual observation. However, such observations would only have been necessary for a limited period of time. Such is the relationship between the orbital characteristics of Venus and the Earth that any appearance of Venus in the light box today would be exactly replicated eight years from today. What is more the phenomenon can only ever take place at specific times of the

The Ecliptic, the Celestial Equator and Sunrise

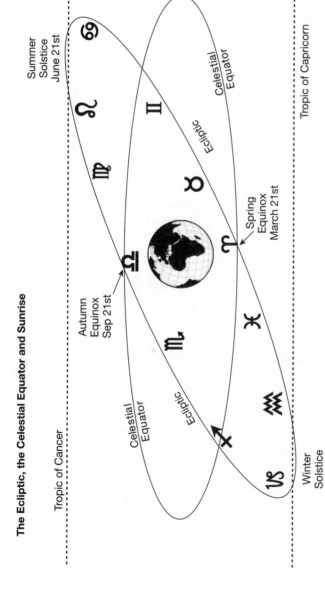

When seen from the Earth the Sun appears to follow a path throughout the year that runs north and south of the celestial equator. This is called the plane of the ecliptic. In reality this reflects the Earths orbit around the Sun. The Earths orbit is tilted relative to the celestial equator and this accounts both for the seasons we experience on Earth and also for the fact that the Sun appears to rise at different points on the eastern horizon throughout the year.

The seats at the east end of the Chapel, looking out over the Glen and almost certainly put there for the purpose of long-term astronomical observation of the eastern horizon

year (between Autumn Equinox and winter solstice and between Spring Equinox and summer solstice.) A further consideration is that for Venus to shine into the light box it must be appearing as a morning star. Once again this cuts down the possibilities to half.

The result is this: Someone would have had to monitor the movements of Venus for an average of about three months each year, for a total of eight years. When Venus appeared in the light box the result would be written down. Eventually a catalogue of such events for the eight-year period would be complete and after this the phenomenon could be predicted with accuracy for centuries to come.

It is interesting to note that the east end of Rosslyn Chapel has stone seats built into the fabric of the building. Before the present retaining wall was built beyond the chapel these seats would have offered an uninterrupted view of the eastern horizon. The seats are most unusual and it is entirely possible that they were included so that in the eight years after the chapel was completed, the necessary observations could be made in relative comfort.

No appearance of either the sun or Venus in the light box would last for long. This is because of the Earth turning on its own axis, though from the perspective of the observer it appears that the sky is constantly passing over our heads. By a simple calculation it can be shown that the sun (and all other heavenly bodies) appears to move across the heavens at a rate of 1° during every four minutes of clock time. If we assume that the solar disc would fit comfortably in the light box when viewed from within the chapel, this means that the light box represents about 0.5° of arc of the heavens. The sun would therefore traverse the light box, when viewed from inside the chapel, in about two minutes of clock time. In reality the light box may be significantly larger but without recourse to very accurate measurements it is presently impossible to say.

One of the facts about the light box that really impressed us was the stunning accuracy that was necessary in aligning the chapel when it was planned and built in the 15th century. Primitive compasses were available at the time, and in fact the principle upon which the compass works was understood long before this period. Vikings, for example, were familiar with the properties of a naturally magnetic iron ore known as 'lodestone'. If a straight piece of lodestone is hung from a piece of twine and allowed to swing freely, one end will always point north and the other south, as with the needle of a modern compass. However, this would have been of little use to the builders of Rosslyn since Magnetic North and True North are not at all the same thing. Because of the peculiarities of the Earth's interior makeup the position of Magnetic North alters across time and can be at odds with True North by a significant amount.

What the builders of Rosslyn were obviously intent upon was building a chapel that had a true and exact east/west alignment and this can only be achieved by very accurate observation and measurement.

The calendar

If we assume that the solar disc, when viewed from within the chapel, fits more or less perfectly in the light box, the accuracy of Rosslyn Chapel's alignment had to be within much less than 0.5° true east/west for the sun, Venus or any other celestial object to stand briefly in the light box on the chosen day. There are a couple of ways this level of accuracy could have been achieved. The architects of Rosslyn Chapel could have established true north by observing the star Polaris and then they would have created an absolutely accurate right angle from this in order to establish True East. Alternatively they could have observed the eastern sky across a period of several years, carefully marking the position of sunrise along the eastern horizon. We know that our ancient Megalithic ancestors were capable of such feats of observation because of the amazing accuracy of the alignments of Megalithic monuments such as Stonehenge and Avebury. Indeed, on Earl William's own land in Orkney there is a burial chamber known as Maes Howe. This also has a light box, carefully constructed above its entrance. It is so cleverly created that when the sun rises at Midwinter it cascades down the tunnel and illuminates the chamber beyond. Maes Howe was built thousands of years before Rosslyn Chapel and stands as testimony to the observational abilities of our remote ancestors.

If we assume that the light box at Rosslyn existed from the time the chapel was constructed, the builders had another problem to contend with. This was the calendar itself.

Because the Earth does not take a uniform 365 days to orbit the sun, but rather 365.25 days, some sort of strategy must be put into place if days within the calendar are not to gradually 'slip' through the year, simply because no calendar can deal with 'part' of a day. In ancient times the Roman Emperor Julius Caser was made very aware of the discrepancies that were building up in the calendar of his period.

Prior to 46 BC the Roman year comprised 12 months, which together equalled 355 days. In addition the Romans added an extra or intercalary month of 22 days on an infrequent basis, between February and March. The calendar worked reasonably well but across time it could be observed that the civil calendar was running at a different rate than the observable year. This was because the Roman year was, on average, 366.25 days in length, a discrepancy of one day each year. Slight refinements were made prior to Julius Caesar's time but these proved to be inadequate. Not only was this making a mockery of religious festivals, many of which had an observable, celestial origin, but planting and harvesting seasons began to appear at the wrong time of year according to the civil calendar. Caesar took advice from the best astronomers of his day and introduced a new sort of calendar. Firstly, to put matters right, he inserted 67 days between November and December of the year 46 BC, together with the additional 23 days that had already been added in the previous February. This meant a total addition to the calendar of 90 days. After this the Romans adopted a year of 365 days, to which an extra day should have been added every fourth year.

Unfortunately something went wrong because the Romans henceforth began to add the extra day every three years. This meant that by the 16th century things had become hopelessly confused again. Now, instead of running behind itself as had been the case in the time of Caesar, the calendar was too advanced, in fact by a period of some ten days. With no Roman Empire to fall back upon the only man in the world who was powerful enough to put things right was the Pope, and so it was Pope Gregory XIII who took on the task of re-ordering the calendar, at least throughout Western Christendom.

Pope Gregory XIII took expert advice and decided that the best way forward was to remove the accumulated 10 days, before instigating a new and more accurate system. His edict was issued for the year 1582. Not all countries accepted his advice, mainly because some states denied his authority. Countries such as the German states and Britain were by this time Protestant and so nominally ignored all rulings from the Vatican. Those countries that did accept the Pope's decree removed the 10 days

Portrait of Pope Gregory XIII (1572–1585) the man who completely revolutionised the calendar

from the civil calendar and then switched to using the calendar that is, more less, still in use to the present day. What resulted was a state of affairs during which travellers not only would have had to adjust their time pieces when they crossed some foreign borders but also their calendars!

Even Protestant countries eventually had to admit that the calendar was hopeless. The German states made the necessary changes in the year 1700 and Britain followed suit in 1752, which to everyone living in Britain was a year of only 355 days. Of course the year 1752 was three centuries after Rosslyn Chapel was built so to Earl William Sinclair and his adviser Sir Gilbert Haye, St Matthew's Day, 21 September, was not the day of the Autumn Equinox, which during their period was taking place on 11 September. We cannot know for certain whether the light box existed in the chapel at the time it was built, or whether it was added during the renovations of the Victorian period, but if it was created with the chapel, Earl William and Sir Gilbert must have been well aware of the discrepancy in the calendar. During their period calls for calendar reform were already taking place across Europe and had been for a number of centuries. As a result they must therefore have orientated the chapel to conform not specifically with 21 September but rather the day of the Autumn Equinox, no doubt realising that once calendar reforms were made, everything would put itself right.

On the other hand, if the light box was not created until the 19th century, when the East Window was rebuilt, this means that it could only be included in the new window because the architects of the chapel had been so scrupulous in their orientation of the building and their knowledge of the inaccurate calendar of their period.

At the time of year we had made our discoveries regarding the light box, 21 September was still some months away. This meant that the only way we could know for certain whether the light box was still working and if so where any light entering it would fall in the chapel, was to recreate the phenomenon for ourselves. With true Indiana Jones zeal we embarked on this experiment in late May and early June of 2006.

12

The experiment

ON 31 MAY 2006 we visited Rosslyn Chapel. As usual these days we found it filled with visitors, many of whom were following the 'Dan Brown trail', identifying the locations used in both the film and the book *The Da Vinci Code*. We took with us the most powerful mobile lamp John had been able to buy, a beast of three million candle-power, and we were anxious to see what would happen when we directed it at the light box above the east window of the chapel.

We wanted to carry out our experiment when the chapel was quiet, partly so as not to disturb other visitors, but also because we had no idea what the result might be. After we had been in the chapel an hour or so there was only one group of visitors present, and they were occupied in the Retro-Choir, which is further east than the great East Window. On the spur of the moment we decided that one of us should go up onto the gantry surrounding the chapel and direct the lamp at the light box. We had decided that in order for our artificial sun to shine directly into the light box it would have to be placed on the end of a pole to give it greater elevation than the gantry could afford. We didn't have the poles with us but we reasoned that at least some of the light would probably fall on our target.

John dutifully climbed the three flights of steel stairs and walked round to the east end of the building, whilst Alan and his wife Kate remained at the west end of the chapel. At most we expected a small glimmer of white light from the lamp to show above the East Window in the comparative gloom of the chapel's interior, but we couldn't have been more wrong. Alan and Kate watched as the light from the lamp played up the crenulated stonework of the window, visible enough through the stained glass on either side, but as the light disappeared from view within the window itself, something totally unexpected happened. Instead of the faint glimmer we had expected to appear in the light box, what met our eyes was a perfect orb of steady, strong, blood red light!

During a changeover between groups of visitors we repeated the exercise and this time Kate directed the lamp from outside, whilst John filmed the result from inside the building. With the building growing busier by the minute there was little more we could do and so we determined to return, as planned, very early the following morning, before the chapel was open to visitors, in order to carry out a more organised experiment.

The result of our efforts on this occasion was somewhat different than had been the case the previous day. Viewed later, in slow motion, we could see that light falling into the exterior of the light box formed, inside the building, what looked like a doughnut of red light, at the centre of which was a much smaller but also brighter spot of white light. As the light source changed its position, the red light became a globe again and it appeared to the naked eye as if the stone itself was beginning to glow red.

Abandoning the interior of the chapel, which was getting busier by the moment, we climbed the gantry once more and concentrated our attention on the outside of the light box. On our earlier photographs we had noticed that there appeared to be light reflecting back from its interior and we were anxious to try and discover why this should be the case. Alan held the lamp on its pole and directed the beam straight into the light box, whilst John filmed the result. What we saw was staggering and absolutely unexpected. It appeared, incongruously, as if more light was being thrown back at us from within the light box than was actually falling into it. Within the box was something that was highly reflective. From our point of perspective some ten feet below the aperture and directly east of the light box, the only way to describe what we saw would be to envisage a surface covered in wrinkled and highly polished aluminium or silver foil. However, when viewed from a more acute angle something different was in evidence. From the right, or the left, it was possible to see that the light box contained something that was heavily faceted, like the surface of a polished gemstone.

At the end of the previous day we had wondered whether the light box was a fairly simple metal lined tube containing a piece of thick, red glass, but it now seemed that it might be far more complex. We burned with curiosity, but at that point there was little more we could achieve. John agreed to return to the chapel at the first possible opportunity to try and establish more and to get better film clips from a tripod-mounted camera, but in the meantime we had more questions than answers. And probably the greatest puzzle of all was trying to understand how whatever lay within the light box, which was intensively reflective, had managed to stay that way for decades. Even if it had been cleaned, or replaced, during the renovations of the 1870s, it had been in place and open to the elements for at least one hundred and thirty years, yet it reflected light so well it looked as though it had been put there only days before. True, Rosslyn Chapel was never subjected to the dust and smog of Britain's industrial past and has a distinctly rural outlook, but one would still have assumed that air-born particles would gradually have accumulated in the entrance to the light box, exposed as it is to the full vent of Scottish gales that regularly batter the chapel.

Still standing on the gantry, we turned to the east. Before us lay the deep, wooded slopes of Rosslyn Glen, a steep-sided valley that falls away directly east. So steep are the sides of the glen, and so close to the chapel, that the crypt is not actually underground at all, but sticks out above the bank side.

The backsight

Beyond the glen lay the rolling scenery of Midlothian. We gazed out, taking in the panorama on this summer day and something we had not noticed or even thought of before occurred to both of us almost simultaneously. In the far distance, maybe some ten miles or so to the east, and directly in line with the where we stood, in front of the East Window, the sides of two hills, one green and one grey, met in a definite and quite pronounced cleft. We repositioned ourselves but there was absolutely no doubt that this cleft in the hills lay absolutely due east of the chapel and its presence began bells ringing in both our minds.

We remembered the life's work of a man whose findings had figured heavily in our research in years gone by. Born in Scotland in 1894, Alexander Thom had been interested in astronomy from an early age, at which time he had acquired an old but powerful telescope. Despite studying engineering at Glasgow University, Thom retained his interest in the heavens and found means, via another love, which was ancient history, to turn his various talents to good use. In his travels throughout Scotland the young Alexander had never failed to take note of the many ancient circles and standing stones that dot the landscape. He studied these carefully and became convinced that they contained, within their placement, important astronomical alignments, regarding both the sun and the moon.

Thom eventually became a professor of engineering at Oxford University in England, but he spent a good percentage of his spare time scrupulously measuring any stone circle or alignment within striking distance. When he retired these efforts became a full-time employment and by the time he died in 1985 he had carefully measured and catalogued perhaps thousands of stone circles, avenues, mounds and alignments from the north of Scotland right down to Brittany in France.

Thom proved conclusively that astronomy was clearly one of the reasons all these sentinels in stone had been erected. Whether for simple calendar awareness or as a result of some religious imperative, our Megalithic ancestors had been great sky-watchers and had left significant evidence of their efforts frozen in stone. Thom observed that in each case, where an alignment existed (for example one that showed the sun rising over a specific stone on the day of the summer or winter solstice), two points of reference were necessary. These he referred to as the 'foresight' and the 'backsight'.

As an example, if we were to stand at the centre of a wide-open piece of ground, with an unobstructed eastern horizon, we might place a stick or a standing stone in the ground, which we would count as our foresight. We would now need another stick or stone, some way off to the east. This would be the backsight. The two would be arranged in such a way so that when an observer stood immediately to the west of the foresight, and lined it up with the backsight in his line of vision, he would be facing that part of the horizon at which the sun would rise on the day of the summer solstice.

Years of patient observation had been necessary in order to create some of the foresights and backsights used in highly complex structures such as Stonehenge and Avebury, both of which are in Wiltshire, England, or at any number of those to be found throughout Scotland, but the principle remains the same. One of the things that Thom also realised was that our ancient ancestors were skilled at placing their structures so that backsights might be quite natural objects. In hilly countryside this may be the tip of a significant hill, a natural spur of rock or the cleft formed in the distance where two hills appear to meet.

As we stood on the gantry at the east end of Rosslyn Chapel on 1 June 2006, we suddenly realised that we were being presented with a backsight of such significance that it was most unlikely to be there by coincidence, or rather that the chapel's position relative to the backsight was not coincidental. The place where we were standing, high on the side of the glen where Rosslyn Chapel had been built, and right in front of the centre of the East Window, was a Spring and Autumn Equinox foresight, for which the cleft in the hills in the distance was the plain and unquestionable backsight.

On the morning of 21 March and 21 September each year, anyone standing in this position and looking to the East would see the disc of the rising sun appear in the notch between the two hills and then climb into the sky.

We had to bear in mind that we were standing high on the artificial gantry, created when the cover was placed over the roof of Rosslyn Chapel. This did not mean that the backsight would be visible from the ground. It didn't take long to establish that this is indeed the case, despite the fact that a fairly high wall has been built around the east side of the Chapel grounds.

It was suggested by those who looked with awe at Rosslyn Chapel back in the 18th and 19th centuries that this building was not the first to be placed on the site. There is a standard and long-standing legend regarding Rosslyn Chapel, though we cannot trace its source, that the site of the chapel was once that of a Mithraic Temple. This is, in fact, extremely unlikely for a number of historical reasons, mainly because it is unlikely that a uniquely Roman temple would ever have been built so far north in Scotland.

The confusion regarding Rosslyn Chapel and its supposed Mithraic connections probably comes about for two reasons. Firstly observers may have been struck by the similarity of style between Rosslyn Chapel itself and Mithraeum that have been excavated elsewhere. The general shape of the building is quite similar and, like all Mithraeum, Rosslyn Chapel has a barrel-vaulted roof. Another reason may be the lack of accurate historical and archaeological knowledge that existed in earlier periods. As an example, Stonehenge, which is probably the most famous of the Megalithic stone circles in England, was regularly referred to in the 18th century as being a Temple of Apollo. This of course would be impossible since Apollo was a Greek deity. The Greeks never settled in England and in any case Stonehenge was completed before Classical Greece even existed.

Despite these obvious confusions, the existence of such a significant backsight to the east of Rosslyn Glen, together with the presence of the chapel there, may well indicate continuity of use. This would not be a unique situation. It was a deliberate policy of early Christians in Britain to occupy sites that were already sacred and to build their churches there, the theory being that worshipers coming to such places would eventually adopt Christianity. Rosslyn Chapel occupies a very elevated and significant position and would have been a logical location for a stone circle or alignment dating back to Megalithic times.

In the following days we turned our attention back to the light box. Since it was impossible to gain access to the light box in Rosslyn Chapel we decided the best way forward would be to create a device that achieved the same observed result. We made an experimental light box from five pieces of Perspex, each 4 inches wide and 2 feet long and covered on one side with mirrored plastic. Turning the mirrored sides in we then fastened the five sides together along their length, to create a pentagonal tube. We now had a highly mirrored tube of the sort that we had observed in the chapel.

We now made two pentangles of Perspex, the same size as the finished tube. Between these we sandwiched a piece of fairly dense but opaque red plastic, leaving a hole in the centre to allow pure light to penetrate the box across an area roughly commensurate with the size of the halogen lamp that was to replicate the rising sun in our experiments. This we taped to one end of the light box.

We now carried out a series of experiments at dead of night in very dark conditions. The light box was placed on a table and we shone the halogen lamp through it at various angles, whilst observing the results from a distance. When the lamp was a few inches below the light box a glimmer of red began to appear in the lower part of the red plastic. This gradually increased in intensity until it glowed a bright and steady blood red in colour. As the light from the lamp climbed further so the white light at the centre of the light box began to show. The red light around it remained in place but appeared diminished by the fierce white light at the centre of the tube. As the lamp was raised still further so the white light disappeared, leaving the blood red doughnut, and this gradually diminished in intensity.

The presence of the mirrored surfaces within the light box intensified and concentrated the light, so that even at a great distance it was impossible to look directly into the light box when the white light was present. The lamp we were using was a small halogen desk lamp and so not a light of particularly great intensity but its power was much magnified by the mirrors.

We took photographs of the result (see colour section) and were satisfied that we had fulfilled most of our objectives. Our observations closely paralleled those we had made at Rosslyn Chapel. The only unknowable was whether or not the Rosslyn light box contains a lens that would concentrate the white light into a tighter beam. Our white light spread out noticeably once it appeared from the end of the light box and if the situation is the same at Rosslyn, it would not light up a specific part of the chapel but rather illuminate the interior at the east end.

Neither can we be sure what form of mirroring is used in the Rosslyn light box. Our experiments indicate something highly reflective, though the result does not look like plain mirrors. John's suggestion that the box may be lined with slabs of polished mica – a highly reflective mineral, may be close to the mark. If the light box is as old as the chapel this would be understandable since mirrors of the modern sort did not exist in the 15th century. Something akin to the modern mirror, in which a sheet of glass is treated with a highly reflective metal, came into use in Venice in the 16th century. Before that mirrors were made from polished metal, such as bronze or tin. As we have already observed, no metal apart from gold would have remained free from oxidisation in the Rosslyn light box and our experiments at the chapel made it seem unlikely that the surfaces were gold plated.

We have done the best we can to explain the remarkable light box at Rosslyn Chapel and at the very least we are bringing it to the attention of those whose responsibility it is to conserve the chapel and to present it to the public. By 21 September 2006 (the next time the sun could contact the light box), this book will be at the printers. We intend to be at the chapel on that morning.

Our experiments indicate that Nancy was correct when she spoke about a white light illuminating the chapel. At the time the solar disc stands squarely in the light box, light emitting from box does indeed turn white. But does it flood into the chapel, illuminating the whole interior, or does the mechanism within the light box create a single beam that lights up a specific part of the chapel? We wait with baited breath, but no matter what might happen, this does not explain exactly why this intricate little machine was built into the fabric of the chapel in the first place.

What we do now know is that the light box has been cunningly created to display a specific pattern in light as the sun rises up the east end of the building on the days of the Spring and Autumn Equinox, as our experiments showed. Not long after dawn the interior of the light box will begin to glow with a steady, red light. This will get brighter as the sun climbs higher into the sky but will eventually recede to form a red ring, within which a much brighter, white light begins to develop. It is likely that this white light becomes so bright that the surrounding red light is blocked out altogether. At its brightest and best the white light cannot enter the chapel for more than three or four minutes, by which time the sun will already occupy an angle that is too steep to directly penetrate the light box. Once again the red ring will appear, followed by the steady red orb, which will eventually fade out as the sun climbs higher and towards the south.

At maximum penetration, the red ring might be compared with the iris of an eye, with the piercing white light being the eye's pupil. All of this is displayed to the interior of the building within a shape that, from the floor of the chapel, looks distinctly triangular. This creates an image that would be familiar to Freemasons and those with an interest in the esoteric and occult. It is known to Freemasons as 'The All Seeing Eye'.

The All-Seeing Eye

The All-Seeing Eye is often portrayed as in the figure below.

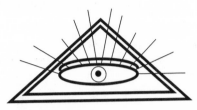

The All-Seeing Eye

It seems to have come into use in Freemasonry in the 17th or possibly the 18th century and at about the same time a similar device had been used in the design of the Great Seal of the United States of America. To Freemasons the All Seeing Eye is nothing more or less than the eye of God himself, or, as they prefer to call the Deity, The Great Architect of the Universe.

In fact the All Seeing Eye has a much older pedigree and undoubtedly evolved from a symbol that was very important to the Ancient Egyptians. This was known as the Eye of Horus.

As the name suggests this symbol is supposed to represent the eye of the god Horus, who was often represented as a hawk. It was the symbol of strength and resurrection.

The Eye of Horus

Is it possible that the light box with its seemingly magical properties was created with the Eye of Horus and the All-Seeing Eye in mind, or did Freemasonry adopt a use of the All-Seeing Eye simply because of its appearance at Rosslyn Chapel?

The light box cannot have been created simply to highlight St Matthew as the dedicatory saint of the chapel, so that worshipers in the chapel below could marvel at the light of the Gospels streaming in on his appointed day, because at the time the chapel was built the inaccurate calendar would have made this impossible. Only after the calendar changes of the 18th century would the Autumn Equinox be seen to take place on 21 September, and therefore coincide with St Matthew's Day.

Were the builders of Rosslyn present in the chapel to see not only the sun shine through the light box, but also the planet Venus? Old versions of the Freemasonic third degree ceremony might indicate a connection. During the third degree the aspirant is ritually killed and laid in a grave. He is drawn forth from the grave by way of a specific 'grip' and raised 'into the light'. At such times it was once common for a five-pointed star shaped light to be placed high in the east, and this would be the first thing the Mason would see when his blindfold was removed. The sun shines into the Rosslyn Chapel light box at dawn, but Venus often does so during the dark hours of night. Unlike any other church we have ever seen, Rosslyn Chapel had shutters mounted outside its lower windows all round the building – despite the fact that we are now certain that the windows contained glass until they were smashed in the late 17th century. Shutters could keep out unwanted light, for example from the moon, but they would also shield whatever was happening inside the chapel from the prying eyes of outsiders.

Were the 'enlightened ones' at Rosslyn taking part in some sort of pre-Masonic ritual under the Shekinah created by the planet Venus shining into the light box? In some precursor of the Masonic third degree ceremony were aspirants introduced to the Mysteries in the Crypt, before being brought up, blindfolded, into the body of the chapel, there to have their blindfold removed under the soft and steady light pouring down onto the chapel's interior? Is this how the first Masons were literally brought 'into the light'?

We cannot know for certain because if there was such a secret it has remained closed and unknown to the modern generation. What remains is the knowledge of a building that must have been planned with meticulous precision, for even an inch or two's error in orientation would have meant the light box working on the wrong days, or not at all. The central tracery of the East Window had to face due east with startling accuracy, something that probably took a long time to get right before building on the chapel could even commence.

By the end of the 18th century the Autumn Equinox and St Matthew's Day had once again been brought together. Worshipers willing to abandon their beds very early on St Matthew's Day could see the miracle of the light box for themselves – though it is highly unlikely that any of them knew how the magic was performed or what it truly meant to the initiated.

13

The birth of Freemasonry

IT IS DIFFICULT to find reliable and consistent evidence for the existence of Freemasonry that extends back beyond the 18th century. Most Freemasons these days more or less accept that Freemasonry developed from the powerful guilds of Stonemasons that go back for centuries. Guilds were a cross between a trade union and a trade federation, in that they served the needs of all levels of workers in a specific craft, from the humblest apprentice to the master and employer. It may also be within the Masonic guilds that we find the history of the secrecy that has always attended Freemasonic practice. It was not in the interest of any guild member to allow the 'mysteries' of his craft to become known beyond its proponents, and fearful oaths sometimes attended the advancement of a craftsman from Apprentice to Journeyman, and from Journeyman to Master, in order to keep the essence of a trade secret and secure.

These days Freemasonry represents a particular form of fraternalism. Members meet on a regular basis and become part of a 'lodge'. Mostly meetings take place in properly appointed buildings, though historically they could take place anywhere, and in particular in the rooms above public houses. Most Freemasons advance through the three established 'degrees' of Freemasonry. These are based on the craft of masonry and upon the semi-legendary stories associated with the building of Solomon's

Temple in Jerusalem. The aspirant has to learn sections of ritual and undergoes ceremonies that take place in a specially created room or temple. Throughout all three degrees he is surrounded by iconography, wears specific clothes and is expected to take oaths dedicated to maintaining the rites and secrets of what is often referred to as 'the Craft'.

Beyond the three established degrees of Freemasonry- those of Entered Apprentice, Fellowcraft and Master- some forms of Freemasonry allow advancement into other degrees. Some of these undoubtedly date back to the earliest forms of Scottish Freemasonry, whilst others are probably much more modern in their creation.

Freemasonry teaches moral rectitude and champions the biblical virtues of Faith, Hope and Love, though it is not, at base, a Christian institution. Any man can become a Freemason and the only religious proviso is that he feels able to express a belief in a deity, which in Freemasonry is usually referred to as 'the Great Architect of the Universe'.

The first known Freemasonic lodges sprang up in Scotland, specifically at a place called Kilwinning, which is not too far from Rosslyn and is a town that stood on Sinclair land. In 1583 a man by the name of William Shaw was appointed by King James VI of Scotland (King James I of England) as 'Master of the Work and General Warden'. This was a post of a very practical Masonic sort – i.e. it specifically dealt with genuine building projects and was not of a 'speculative' nature, as modern Freemasonry is said to be. In 1598 William Shaw drew up a statute that set out the duties and responsibilities of the 'operative' lodge, the better to organise the stonemasons of Scotland. Later, in 1589, Shaw created another statute and this is the one that interests Freemasons because it made a veiled reference to 'speculative' Freemasonry (speculative Freemasons are not associated with the art of dressing or erecting stone buildings.) The second Shaw statute bore reference to the claim that the Mother Lodge of Scotland was at Kilwinning. Shaw instructed all Masonic lodges to keep good and accurate records, and as a result he is seen by many as being the father of modern Freemasonry.

Other lodges proliferated in Scotland, not least amongst them that of Roslin. The Sinclairs of Roslin became the hereditary Grand Masters of Scottish Freemasonry, a role they maintained even after Grand Lodge of Scotland was founded in 1736 when William St Clair of Roslin became the first Grand Master under Grand Lodge.

The first known initiation of a Freemason in England was that of Sir Robert Moray in 1641, followed by that of Elias Ashmole in 1646. It is thought that Freemasonry became quite popular in England after this date but problems associated with the Crown of England and the Jacobite uprisings forced it underground, mainly because Freemasons became synonymous with the cause of the Catholic Stuart kings, whilst England opted for a German protestant king.

In 1717 four lodges located at various public houses throughout the city of London came together to form The Premier Grand Lodge of England, and Freemasonry rapidly recreated itself and its practices to suit the political needs of England. In the meantime Freemasonry had found its way to other places, particularly the dependent English colonies in North America. When these infant states fell out with England, an event that led to the American War of Independence, Freemasonry was in the vanguard of the patriots and many of the American generals, including George Washington, were high ranking Freemasons. It is for this reason that the US has sometimes been referred to as the first Masonic State, and Masonic iconography still lies at the heart of US government.

Freemasonry has never had a very good working relationship with the established Catholic Church. The Church thought and still thinks that it would be impossible to be both a practising Freemason and a committed Catholic. In any case the Church fell out with Freemasonry during the time of the French Revolution, and the breach has never been satisfactorily healed.

Some branches of Freemasonry, of which there are many, ally themselves to the Knights Templar, and consider that Freemasonry is the direct legatee of the Templar order, though as we have pointed out that there is no direct evidence to support this theory.

Freemasonry continues to be a fraternal organisation that enjoys significant patronage across the world. It works tirelessly and generally quietly to raise large sums of money for charities, is now less secretive than it ever was and professes no political intention. Indeed Freemasons these days are expected to put the needs of their family and those of their nation before that of the Craft.

It is our belief that Freemasonry is not simply 'associated' with Rosslyn Chapel but rather that it owes its existence to the building. Freemasonry is not a religion. Its working principles are philosophical. Anyone who takes the trouble to look deep within the Craft will see that at its heart Freemasonry is a direct legatee of the rising humanism and deism that was beginning to spread across Western Europe during the 15th century and which typified the later Renaissance – but it is also much more.

The Temple

At the very centre of Freemasonic ritual and practice is Solomon's Temple, a structure created three thousand years before the first Freemason is mentioned in any document; a building that even in its most recent incarnation was destroyed around 100 AD. Although the vast majority of Freemasons remain unaware of the fact, Freemasonry is also filled to the brim with carefully veiled reference to astronomy – in fact the American Mason Robert Hewit Brown in his 1882 book *Stella Theology and Masonic Astronomy* aptly and convincingly shows that practically every single aspect of Freemasonic symbolism or practice is cosmological in origin. Hewit Brown also demonstrates a rich skein of Kabalism within Masonic ritual.

There are several specific places within the Chapel where Freemasons are directed in order to establish a tangible connection between the Craft and the ornamentation of the building. Some of the connections made are tenuous, such as the supposed head of the murdered apprentice, whose presence is said to relate to the story of the Apprentice Pillar and the fury of the Master Mason mentioned in Chapter 1. A close examination of the carved head in question demonstrates that it has been deliberately and badly altered at some stage after its creation. The face quite obviously once possessed a beard, which has been inexpertly hacked off, most likely to make the face look younger. What is almost certain to have happened in this case is that the story of the murdered apprentice arose at some unspecified date and that to substantiate it the head of an Old Testament patriarch was altered.

However, there is one carving in the chapel that does relate directly to Freemasonry and which cannot be so easily explained. On the lower frame of the window in the south west corner of the chapel there is a carving that, judging by its condition, is absolutely contemporary with the chapel's creation. It does not appear to have been altered in any way. It

The carving from the Chapel that is said by Freemasons to depict the third degree ceremony of initiation

depicts a blindfolded figure kneeling between two pillars. His feet are in an odd configuration, he has a noose around his neck and in his left hand he is holding what is clearly meant to be a Bible. The loose end of the rope that emanates from the noose is being held by another figure, standing behind the first. The figure that wears the blindfold and noose is dressed similarly to a candidate who is undergoing the first degree ceremony of Freemasonry, in which the pillars, the blindfold, the noose and the Bible all still play a part.

Other aspects of the chapel show a relationship with Freemasonry, some of which come from our own unique research. A good example is the presence of the three pillars used on Masonic first degree tracing boards and their close connection with the three pillars at the east end of the chapel – an association that indicated an understanding of and reverence for the Kabala in each case. Most telling of all is the light box and the way it creates that all-important light high in the east – the reflected and amplified light of the planet Venus that was once central to the Masonic third degree ritual.

The first Freemasons

One plausible explanation for the origins of Freemasonry is that the Craft was deliberately and carefully created as an adjunct to the chapel. Our evidence has demonstrated that Earl William Sinclair and Sir Gilbert Haye were believers in a form of Christianity that, during the 15th century, would have been considered heretical. They also delved into the equally dangerous world of humanism and of the Kabala. Rosslyn Chapel was built in the knowledge of these beliefs, and to record them – but only to those who could read the most intimate volumes of the library in stone.

Even before the chapel was completed, times were changing in a religious sense. The erstwhile humanistic and liberal popes of the middle 15th century gave way to a series of reactionary popes, whose backward-looking, intolerant and dictatorial attitudes would soon lead to a split within the Western Church and to the horrible wars that attended the Reformation.

The Earl was faced with a problem. How would it be possible to pass on knowledge of the timeless truths carved into the walls of the chapel, without divulging its secrets to the world at large and thereby bringing retribution down on his own head and that of his children? The creation of Freemasonry was his response.

Some of his most elevated craftsmen, his stone-carvers and the artists who so colourfully enhanced their work, were men of intelligence, perhaps brought from as far away as Italy and paid commensurate with their great skills. The labourers on site, the stone cutters and dressers and those who had laboured so long over the foundations and the possible vault that lay below the chapel were probably more local in origin but all those on the site became part of the same family. Working and living for decades in the same place their families would have intermarried and had children, some of whom themselves grew to work on the project. They would become, in every real sense of the word, a brotherhood.

Utilising this sense of common purpose and allying it to the naturally secretive and insular nature of the guild system, Earl William created a unique institution at Rosslyn. Its existence ensured the silence of his workers – especially those who were party to the building's most intimate secrets. Although designed around guild practices, particularly those of the already existent guild of stonemasons, the Earl's fraternity also carried the same truths that his workers were carving into the chapel walls. These truths were expressed in ritual and couched in allegory. Everyone from lowest to highest learned the same words, wore the same ritual clothing and performed the same rites, but only those who proved themselves to be trustworthy and steadfast would ever have come to understand what all the strange words and gestures actually meant.

This new fraternity brought all the benefits of the guilds. If a worker grew sick he was supported. If he died, his family were looked after and his children were educated and given a trade.

Access to this very important self-help fraternity came at a price. It was secret and so horrible oaths were created, promising dire retribution to anyone who divulged the smallest of its secret rituals or practices. And in an age in which violence, lawlessness and retribution were endemic, such oaths would be taken very seriously indeed.

Members of the club could recognise each other by use of specific grips and handshakes, as well as phrases and gestures that outsiders could not recognise. Doubtless these first Freemasons met in the stone-built chapel down the hill to the west of the present building. It was erected at

The ruins of the former Chapel of St Matthew, only a stone's throw away from the present Chapel and now the site of a graveyard

some time prior to the commencement of Rosslyn Chapel and two of its stout stone buttresses can still be seen in St Matthew's cemetery. To the 'brothers' this would have been Church and Temple combined.

With the passing of Earl William in 1480, responsibility for the still unfinished chapel devolved to one of his sons, Oliver, who inherited the Roslin lands and title. He finished roofing the chapel and completed the west wall. If the chapel was ever really intended to form part of a much bigger church, neither Oliver nor his successors did anything about it. Contemporary records show that the Sinclairs continued to use the chapel for their own devotions, which in the case of the family took place not in the body of the building but rather in the Crypt. The Sinclair lords continued to be buried within the chapel, in the family vault located somewhere beneath it.

Meanwhile the Earl's own particular brand of Freemasonry flourished and spread. Part of its original inspiration may have come from that peculiar brand of reformed Benedictine monks, the Tironensians (see

The foundation stones that once supported the bridge from the Castle to the old village of Roslin

Chapter 2).The Tironensians were great architects and stonemasons. One of their most prestigious abbeys stood on Sinclair land, at Kilwinning, and this is the place that claimed to have oldest of all Freemasonic Lodges, which was called 'Lodge o'.

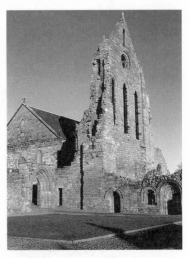

With the chapel as complete as it would ever be, the fraternity that had built it seems to have been unwilling to disband. Soon people were joining the 'club' who had never chiselled a stone in their life. These were the first 'speculative' Freemasons.

Despite changes in ritual and form, at least some of the original secrets of Freemasonry still exist – if one is

The stately ruins of Kilwinning Abbey, a Tironensian foundation on Sinclair land

sufficiently well versed in astronomy, ancient religion and mythology to tease them out. Many of them don't even seem much like secrets to the modern observer, but then of course we live in a very different age. (Publicly declaring that the Earth circles the sun would have spelled certain death when Rosslyn Chapel was built.) And at the heart of Freemasonry we still find imperatives that were critically important to William Sinclair and Gilbert Haye. These include a deep reverence for John the Baptist, an enduring belief in justice, equality and fraternity, a reverence for the Noahide Laws of ancient Judaism and a recognition (though hardly any Freemasons realise it these days) for that all-important part of the year around the Autumn Equinox.[19]

Taking all considerations into account it seems that Rosslyn Chapel was not just significant to Freemasonry, it was crucial. The same heady cocktail of Old Testament legend, Ebionite Christianity, mystery-rite religion and a reverence for the human spirit that were personified by the 15th century Sinclairs was passed directly to Freemasonry and, in part, survives with the Craft to this day.

---

19 See *The Goddess, the Grail and The Lodge* and *The Virgin and the Pentacle* by Alan Butler.

Long after interest in *The Da Vinci Code* has waned Freemasons from around the world will still be making their way to Rosslyn Chapel. And that is how it should be, because without this extraordinary building Freemasonry would never have existed. Rosslyn Chapel is without any doubt the oldest and most important of all Freemasonic Temples.

14

Fiction or fact?

WE NOW COME to two of the most important and controversial traditions relating to Rosslyn Chapel. Firstly there is the suggestion, accepted by many, that the Chapel has a strong association with the Knights Templar and that it might even have been built by the Templars. Secondly there is the widespread belief that the Chapel has a secret vault far below its floors, and that this contains some unspecified treasure.

The suggestion that Rosslyn Chapel was either planned or built directly by the Knights Templar is clearly at odds with the historical information available and is simply not tenable. The Templars were effectively destroyed in 1307 (and across the following five years) by the French monarch, Philip IV and his tame pope, Clement V. Although there are traditions that Templar knights were protected in Scotland after their persecution elsewhere, this is not borne out by the available evidence. It is true that measures taken against Templars in England and Scotland were far more half-hearted than had been the case in France, but the order was disbanded in both countries. A few Templars were prosecuted in England and others, in both England and Scotland, retired into Cistercian monasteries. What is more, there is evidence that the Sinclairs actually testified against the Templars in Scotland. At a trial held in 1308, which was headed by William

A grave slab now kept in the Chapel and said to denote the Templar credentials of William St Clair. In fact the design merely demonstrates his title of Earl and his aristocratic position in society. It has no relationship to the Knights Templar

de Lamberton, Bishop of St Andrews, both Earl Henry Sinclair and his son William suggested that 'If the Templars had been in any way faithful Christians, they would in no way have lost the Holy Land.' Sinclairs are also known to have subsequently taken former Templar land as their own.

Even if any Templars had managed to survive in Scotland for another century and a half, for which there is no historical proof, they would surely have had no truck with a family that had contributed directly to their downfall as a religious order in Scotland.

But there is every indication that the Sinclairs had once got on very well with the Templars, and we surely cannot judge their actions after 1307 as being indicative of their allegiances across the two hundred years of Templar existence. In any case, by 1308 the Templars were a lost cause. The Sinclairs could have gained nothing and might have lost much if they had chosen to champion the Templars in the Scottish legal proceedings.

The disappearance of an organisation doesn't mean the disappearance of the beliefs that led to its creation. In Chapter 6 we outlined the very strong evidence of a wide-ranging and orchestrated series of events that took place between the 11th and the 14th centuries, all of which emanated from Champagne – evidence of a major schism that was taking place at the heart of Western Christianity. These were the events that had led to the First Crusade and to the creation of a number of institutions that between them would reshape the very fabric of Western Europe. One of these agencies was the Knights Templar. The most likely scenario is that the rulers of Champagne in the 11th century were surviving members of Ebionite families, which had escaped from Jerusalem sometime after 70 AD and who had flourished further west. Their demonstrable intention was to seize Jerusalem and to re-establish there what they considered to be the 'rightful' and 'original' religion that had been perverted into Catholicism. There, in Jerusalem, they would re-establish the line of Davidic priests of which John the Baptist and Jesus had been two examples.

This is in fact what very nearly happened. The Western Kings who took power in Jerusalem after the First Crusade came from families that had strong dynastic ties to the Counts of Champagne. But these rulers always had a major problem, this being that the number of Ebionite families in Europe was limited. They had mobilised the whole of Western and much of Eastern Christianity to wrest the Holy Land from the Muslims but they were not themselves sufficiently numerous to hold it. When Western interest in crusading waned, even the ranks of the Templars could not hold back the inevitable onslaught and the result was that Jerusalem was recaptured by the Muslims in 1187 and Western forces were driven altogether from the Holy Land by the end of the 13th century. It was this eventuality that, in part, led to the destruction of the Knights Templar, an institution that became a scapegoat for Western failures to hold the Near East.

However, in the 12th century things had been very different. In 1118 when the first Templar knights had travelled to Jerusalem, their own greatness and that of their cousins the Cistercians lay in the future. Hugh de Payen and his companions may have been the vanguard of what was to come, but they could have had no way of knowing if their ultimate strategy would succeed and whether Jerusalem would become for ever the true home of the Ebionite faith.

The persistent rumours that what Hugh and his colleagues were actually doing in Jerusalem for nine years was digging excavations survive down to the early days of Freemasonic ritual. Within old versions of Scottish rite Freemasonry there are very specific accounts of the excavation made by Hugh de Payen and the other Templar Knights beneath the Temple Mound and of what they discovered there. The account is to be found in the degree of 'The Holy Royal Arch'. Couched in symbolic terms, relating to the second Temple in Jerusalem and the priest Zerubbabel, is a blow by blow account of what was clearly a carefully orchestrated 12th century archaeological dig. The ritual leaves no doubt that important treasures, specifically documents, were found and recovered.

If this ritual is the recounting of a genuine event, and it certainly reads as such, the first Templars really did either stumble across something of importance – or else knew full well what to look for as a result of safely-guarded traditions handed down across the generations. But what happened to the booty henceforth?

Further Masonic traditions, this time from Kilwinning in Scotland, the oldest of all Scottish lodges, gives details that mesh well with the information in the Holy Royal Arch degree. The Kilwinning story goes as follows:

Around the year 1140 the Pope encouraged groups of Italian stone-masons, who were the most accomplished in Europe, to travel to other lands, in order to beautify the churches there. He specifically organised these craftsmen into 'lodges' one of which came to Kilwinning in Scot-land in order to build a new monastery there. They brought with them the important and supposedly ancient records of their lodge, and these were subsequently deposited in the Abbey of Kilwinning.

This story can be shown to be inaccurate for a couple of reasons. Firstly there is no record of any pope offering such instructions or creating any sort of Masonic lodge. Secondly, Kilwinning abbey was not built by foreign craftsmen. We can be certain of this because Kilwinning abbey was founded by the same group of stone-working monks mentioned in Chapter 2 – the Tironensians. Not only did the Tironensians build all their own abbeys, they were also so proficient in masonry that they completed many tasks for other agencies too. No foreign lodge of masons would have been either necessary or tolerated. But one can easily see how the real story became distorted. The masons who built Kilwinning abbey were from abroad, because monks from the Mother house in France were involved in the construction of the new abbey. And in a way they were sanctioned by the Pope because the Tironensians were an established monastic order.

Despite the inaccuracy of the Kilwinning legend, there could be an important clue here. The story asserts that ancient and important documents were placed in the new Abbey of Kilwinning, a foundation that stood on lands owned by the Sinclair Earls. Of equal interest is the fact that another Tironensian abbey, at Kelso, was founded in 1128, and this is exactly the same year as the first Templars returned from Jerusalem; when they were made an official order and when they gained lands in Scotland. Our suggestion is as follows:

Important documents, probably very much akin to those comprising the Dead Sea Scrolls that were discovered in the 1940's in caves above the Essene settlement of Qumran, close to the River Jordan, were found by the Templar knights during their excavations of the Temple ruins in Jerusalem. It's not so improbable- they were, after all, nearly 1,000 years closer to the early Christians than we are, and much has come to light by chance discovery in the last century. These documents were deemed to be so important (perhaps because they itemised the truth about John the Baptist and the Ebionite Davidic line), that they were taken as far from the seat of ecclesiastical power and the grasping hands of European monarchs as possible. In 1128, when Hugh de Payen and his colleagues are known to have travelled to Scotland, the documents were brought to the safest and most distant outpost they could devise.

There the Tironensian monks, a monastic order as closely related to the Templars as were the Cistercians, built an abbey at Kelso, specifically to house the documents. It subsequently became obvious that Kelso was too close to the English border and it was feared that the abbey might be ravished in some future battle between the Scots and English. As a result, in 1140, the Tironensians embarked upon the building of yet another abbey, this one at Kilwinning, further away from any possible English incursion. The documents were moved from Kelso to Kilwinning and deposited there in 1140, where they were also under the supervision of the Sinclairs, who as the protectors of the 'Holy Shining Light' had been Ebionites all along.

By the 15th century circumstances ordered themselves in such a way that it became possible to create a custom-built temple to house the documents – a place with immensely deep and strong vaults that would never be penetrated. This was Rosslyn Chapel. Admittedly much of what we are suggesting here is speculation, but the dates fit and the pivotal information that makes all of this credible relates to the Tironensians, whose significance regarding these matters has never been examined before.

Another, perhaps associated explanation for Rosslyn Chapel as a treasure house emerges at a date much closer to the building of the Chapel. It specifically relates to Sir Gilbert Haye and the part he personally played in the planning and building of Rosslyn.

Gilbert Haye and Rene d'Anjou

During the period in which Rosslyn Chapel was planned and built, new incentives and ideas were developing within European society. Philosophy was gradually eroding religious dogma, free and wide-ranging discussion was being positively championed and the notion of chivalry was being elevated to an art form. Nowhere was this more evident than at the court of a man who held the title of King of Naples, but who during his lifetime was also Duke of Anjou, Count of Provence, Count of Piedmont, Duke of Bar, Duke of Lorraine. Most telling of all he was the titular King of Jerusalem, a title that had been maintained and passed on lineally, even after Jerusalem had been wrested from Christian control. The title 'King of Jerusalem' still existed by the 15th century and had passed to those who had also eventually came to the Kings of Naples. The King in question was Rene d'Anjou. Together with his mother, Yolande of Aragon, one of the shrewdest and most influential women ever to hold temporal power in Europe, Rene would prove to be perhaps the most important and elevated prince of his age. It is a mark of respect to his enlightened attitude, cultured bearing and natural charm that even after five centuries he is still referred to as 'Good King Rene'.

To say that Rene lived in interesting times is something of an understatement. He was born in 1409, with the blood of the Counts of Champagne running in his veins. He amassed his amazing array of titles during an eventful life. Nurtured and safeguarded by his Mother, Yolande of Aragon, Rene was partly responsible for Charles VII, his brother in law, gaining the French crown in 1429. Charles' coronation had come at the end of a long struggle against the English, who due to an earlier treaty considered the throne of France to be theirs. Both Yolande and Rene had supported the extraordinary Joan of Arc, who inspired and led the French knights. The idea of any peasant leading an army, let alone an illiterate young woman, would have been unthinkable to feudal Europe but Yolande and Rene were remarkable people. Yolande was the Queen of four kingdoms, and had brought up the infant Charles as her own. As a result she wielded great influence over the young King, whilst Rene and King Charles were like brothers.

Rene d'Anjou was no ordinary aristocrat. In great part he is responsible for the Renaissance, not just on account of his own amassing of manuscripts and his sponsorship of artists but chiefly because he also encouraged others to do likewise. Rene knew the Medici in Florence and it was him who encouraged Cosimo de Medici to send out emissaries across the known world to locate manuscripts that would fill the shelves of the San Marco library – the first public library in the world! Rene was cultured, urbane, charming and quick to recognise anyone's potential,

Portrait of King Rene d'Anjou as an old man by Nicolas Froment

no matter what their rank or station. He spoke several languages, was a prolific writer himself and showed a definite interest in alchemy and the Kabala. At his court he had a Jewish astrologer and an expert on the Kabala whose name was Jean de Saint Remy. This man was the grandfather of the much more famous Nostradamus.

Both Yolande and Rene were present at the coronation of King Charles VII, as indeed was Sir Gilbert Haye. Rene and Gilbert must have known each other well because their paths crossed many times and they had much in common. They were both fascinated with chivalry and with the concept of responsible kingship. In addition they were both natural philosophers and keen historians. Rene d'Anjou was lucky to be living during the pontificates of men such as Pope Nicholas V and Pope Paul II, men who shared his love of literature and who looked the other way regarding some of his quite peculiar beliefs, some of which centred on both Mary Magdalene and St John the Baptist, not to mention his championing of the Kabala.

Is it possible that Rene had inherited more than his genes from Champagne? Endowed as he was with the title 'King of Jerusalem' was he a legatee of the Jerusalem Church? Could Rene have been a leader of the Ebionite lineage?

During the long years Gilbert Haye spent as librarian to the King of France, he would have corresponded regularly with Rene d'Anjou and would have met him frequently. In his work Gilbert had access to some of the most important and amazing manuscripts available anywhere and he undoubtedly also obtained copies of works in Rene's own collections, the better to expand the French king's library. Rene and Gilbert's personal fascination with chivalry and with Aristotle's supposed correspondence with Alexander the Great, as well as with the romance stories popular at the time, such as those relating to King Arthur, would have made them natural soul-mates.

We know that when Gilbert Haye came to Rosslyn in 1456 he had with him many manuscripts, but the only ones we can name are those that have survived to grace the shelves of public libraries and private collections. We see it as highly likely that some of the material Gilbert Haye brought back from France had either been obtained from Rene d'Anjou or else copied from works in Rene's own vast library. The most prized possessions would have been a copy of the original St Matthew Gospel in Hebrew and perhaps other documents from the Ebionite fathers. As titular King of Jerusalem and the direct legatee of Godrey de Bouillon and his brother King Baudoin of Jerusalem, Rene is most likely to have had such documents in his possession. These too could quite easily have found their way to Scotland, to be placed with reverence alongside the earlier documents in the vault below the Chapel.

As a good indication that such documents did exist, there is a surviving story that tells of a near disastrous fire that took place in Rosslyn Castle in 1447, at a time when work on the fabric of Rosslyn Chapel had been underway only a year. The story runs as follows:

*'About this time (1447) there was a fire in the square keep (of Rosslyn
Castle) by occasion of which the occupants were forced to flee the building.
The Prince's chaplain, seeing this, and remembering all of his master's
writings, passed to the head of the dungeon where they all were, and
threw out four great trunks where they were. The news of the fire coming
to the Prince through the lamentable cries of the ladies and gentlewomen,
and the sight thereof coming to his view in the place where he stood upon
Colledge Hill, he was sorry for nothing but the loss of his Charters and
other writings; but when the chaplain who had saved himself by coming
down the bell rope tied to a beam, declared how his Charters and Writts
were all saved, he became cheerful and went to recomfort his Princess
and the Ladys.*[20]

It would be strange indeed if a man of the Earl's compassion and kindness
displayed more concern for his legal documents than for his own wife
or the other ladies of the court, but the whole story becomes far more
understandable if he had briefly thought that documents of incalculable
worth had gone up in flames.

The only absolute proof of the existence of a secret vault below Rosslyn
Chapel would come with a careful and well-organised search, complete
with modern ground-scanning radar and the sophisticated archaeological
techniques now available. Perhaps understandably the present trustees of
Rosslyn Chapel are reticent to sanction such an undertaking. It is difficult
to see what they could have to gain by doing so. The Chapel is open to
the public and is expected to support itself financially. Rumours about
treasure are always appealing and ensure high visitor numbers. However, if
anything significant were to be found at Rosslyn it would most probably
be taken off to some museum, leaving Rosslyn Chapel like the empty tomb
of some ancient Egyptian Pharaoh, with its once great treasure missing.
If, on the other hand, nothing was found below the Chapel, much of the
mythos would evaporate and the cash registers on the entry gate and in
the souvenir shop would be quieter than they are at present.

We remain open-minded about the possibility, though our recent
investigations have bolstered rather than diminished the possibility that
there are indeed documents beneath the Chapel, and we are tantalisingly

---

20 Wallace-Murphy T: *An Illustrated Guide to Rosslyn Chapel.* Publisher and date unknown.

close to demonstrating that something even more significant than documents may also be hidden there. However this does nothing to make us lose sight of the fact that the real treasure of Rosslyn Chapel is available to anyone who has the chance to walk around this 15th century masterpiece.

15

Changing times

IN 1456 THE area around Rosslyn Castle must have been a hive of activity.

The village of Rosslyn that had existed for centuries on the east side of Rosslyn Glen was abandoned and a new village was commenced to the west of the chapel site. There Earl William brought together the artists and workmen necessary to build the chapel. The Earl would have been well aware that although there was a relaxation of Church dogma apparent at the time, this was a situation that could change at almost any moment. Being intimately associated with its construction, his workers could hardly fail to recognise some of its secrets, for example the light box over the East Window or the deep chambers that lay below the chapel. It was imperative that William secured both their loyalty and secrecy if he was to avoid some of the chapel's most intimate details becoming common knowledge. This is when the Earl hit upon a way of ensuring the confidentiality of his workers that would lead to the creation of Freemasonry (see Chapter 13). William's efforts in this direction were made easier by the fact that Sir Gilbert Haye had written several books relating to the guild system. He discussed these in his translation of *The Buke of the Law of Armss or the Buke of Bataillis*, a translation of Honore Bonet's *Arbre des batailles*.

Times changed in Scotland when the 15th century came to an end.

The rising forces of Protestantism and the religious wars that the Reformation inspired across Europe were facts of life from which even remote Scotland could not be immune. The Catholic Church gradually lost its grip on the far north-west of Europe and the increasingly stagnant rigidity of its dogma was supported by force of arms. Catholicism was replaced by Protestantism, but the stark monochromes of the new faith sought to obliterate the mystery and magic of Catholicism. Paradoxically it was hidden within the ornamentation, the relics and the statuary of Catholicism that Ebionite beliefs had managed to survive. Protestantism, together with the arrival of the Age of Reason, should have offered the Ebionites their first opportunity for centuries to practice their own beliefs openly, but unfortunately their freedom was even more eroded and proscribed. This may be one of the reasons why the Freemasonic path proved to be so important. It represented a way to carry the message of John the Baptist and the Ebionites forward in secret, though apparently divorced from any established Church – Catholic or Protestant.

The Chapel was used by the Sinclairs of Rosslyn throughout the 16th century, but the apparent Catholicism of the family made them unpopular and they eventually had no choice but to fall in line with the status quo. Eventually they were forced to destroy the altars in Rosslyn. A later family member, Sir Simon Sinclair, was exiled to Ireland for practicing what was said to be a family mass in the Chapel. If he had not had such a family history of service to the Scottish Crown, there is little doubt he would have been executed.

Rough treatment was handed out to Rosslyn Castle and the chapel by Cromwell's troops under General Monk in 1650, in which the Castle was as good as destroyed, but the Chapel famously and miraculously spared. Then came another attack by a Protestant mob on 11 December 1688. The unruly assembly arrived at ten in the evening. It is said that in addition to doing some damage to the Chapel this mob also broke into the castle and stole the original manuscript of Adam Abel associated with the extant *Le Miroir de l'Humaine Salvation.*

With the passing of time the chapel itself fell into disrepair – its windows were broken and birds nested amongst the carvings. Some attempts were made to repair it during the 18th century, but was it was Sir John Clerk of Penicuik who began Rosslyn's first real renewal in about 1747. However, it was not really until the Victorian era that interest generated by Queen Victoria and the nobility prompted a thorough restoration. By this time the chapel and its attendant title had passed out of the original Sinclair family and into a family that became known as Erskine-Sinclair, the original Sinclairs of Rosslyn having died out in the male line. The Erskine Sinclairs became the first Earls of Rosslyn. The newcomers were not privy to hereditary secrets of the direct line. An example of this occurred with the death of the 2nd Earl of Rosslyn in 1837. The Earl had left instructions that he wished to be buried in the ancient vault. A frantic search was made of the floor of the Chapel, but to quote M'Dowall's guidebook of the 1860s '...*the attempt was not attended by success, as hitherto it had been a century past, completely unknown, and not a trace of it visible. The Earl was therefore interred near the remains of his Countess who died in 1810*'.

People without this rudimentary information can surely not have been party to the deepest knowledge of the chapel, which seems to have died with the male line of the original Sinclair family. Only a rising interest in Freemasonry carried at least a few of the chapel's secrets forward into the future, but even Freemasons did not possess the necessary key to connect their Craft to the unique religious and philosophical imperative that lay at the heart of this most remarkable building.

The 3rd and 4th Earls of Rosslyn, both Freemasons, and especially the 4th Earl, began a restoration programme that saw the recreation of the altars in 1862. These had been designed by David Bryce for the 3rd Earl. The restoration and redesigning of the great East Window came in 1871 and the building of the baptistery was started in June 1880 by Andrew Kerr for the 4th Earl. The baptistery took six months to build and cost £758/8/6d. This was followed by the replacement of the stained glass clerestory windows in 1887. So even though most of the Sinclair hereditary knowledge of the direct line had faltered, the love of the building, an appreciation of its significance and a responsibility for the restoration of the Chapel's unique beauty were taken very seriously by the Victorian Earls of Rosslyn.

Today the Chapel is run by a trust, and although it is open to the public as a place of interest, it is also used as a Christian Church. Work to keep the Chapel standing goes on and more ambitious renovations are planned for the future. Thus it is hoped that this most remarkable of late-medieval gems will delight and astonish visitors well into the future.

In conclusion

We are well aware that despite the years of research we have already put into Rosslyn Chapel that there is still much more to learn. For example; our initial rediscovery of the light box at the Chapel's east end has alerted us to many other possibilities regarding the use of the building as an astronomical observatory. All of the eastern horizon, from North to South, can be seen as an uninterrupted panorama from the east end of the Chapel. Whilst the light box was clearly created to highlight astronomical happenings that take place due east, the option would have been open to observe much more than these limited events. Does the Chapel contain foresights and backsights that line up with the other important corners of the year – summer and winter solstice? Our initial findings in this direction are promising but more work is needed in order to be certain.

Whilst we now have a good understanding of what many of the carvings inside and outside the Chapel are trying to tell us, there are still many whose meanings we cannot comprehend. The stone cubes mentioned in Chapter 10 are a good case in question. Putting aside for a moment the possibility that these are some sort of musical notation, we wonder if they rather represent deliberately created hieroglyphs – perhaps the index to this library in stone?

More work is required regarding the physical shape and dimensions of the building. We know it was built using a 'double rectangle' ground plan, of the sort that was common in ancient temples, and we are further intrigued by the arrangement of the internal pillars, the number of external pinnacles, the most unusual barrel-vaulted roof and the possible original purpose of the roof over the Retro-Choir. What have we yet to learn about the Crypt, and how much more than we have presently understood might those strange and enigmatic Tironensian monks, with their Culdean nature-orientated beliefs, have figured in the planning and building of the Chapel?

There is also more to learn about the remarkable Sir Gilbert Haye and the part he actually played in the planning and building of Rosslyn Chapel. We are presently researching new information regarding Sir Gilbert that may well turn out to be the definitive reason for the existence of the enigma that is Rosslyn Chapel but before we can commit this to paper there will be journeys to undertake and more ancient documents to analyse.

To sum up, we see Rosslyn Chapel as being very much a creation of the schismatic religious beliefs of its creators. These were people who clearly had a deep and abiding 'faith'. Their personal slant on religion was much affected by aspects of the remote animistic past, as well as ideas that were surfacing as the first glow of the Renaissance was starting to illuminate a Europe that had been darkened so long by Church dogma and feudal government.

There is something deeply surprising about the Chapel's acceptance of mythical and religious truths from across such a vista of time and geographical area. Within and without its walls we can recognise images that must have originated from as far away as distant China; there are others that seem to point to Indian sources and still more that clearly come not only from the Middle East but from a Middle East so ancient that its burgeoning beliefs lie deep at the heart of the human psyche.

We can be certain that no single overriding religious belief dominates in this sacred spot. At the moment it is used as a Christian Church but the building itself is a testimony to the fact that all gods are the same God, whether or not its modern worshipers accept the fact.

Freemasonry, whether you love it, hate it, or are indifferent, helped shape our world between the 18th and the 20th centuries, but that's a separate subject. We do believe though that it owes its very existence to Rosslyn Chapel and its founders. But visiting Freemasons cannot adopt the Chapel as being uniquely their own. There is something for every believer here, in what was clearly intended to be a compendium of religious and philosophical thought.

Above all the promise of Paradise that was the Kingdom of Heaven on Earth is represented in stone in Rosslyn, epitomised in the stone tree, which in the early 1800s, erroneously became known as the Apprentice Pillar. Displayed in the carvings in the upper branches of the heavenly tree are angels of all the classifications. All nine Celestial Orders are represented. These are Seraphin, Cherubin, Thrones, Dominions, Virtues, Powers, Principalities, Archangels and Angels. Many of the carvings represent specific Angels like Michael, Gabriel and Metatron. Also present are the governing angels of the four seasons. Spring – Spugliguel, Summer -Tubiel, Autumn -Torquaret, Winter – Attarib. These are to be found within the four seasonal vines. The angels of the twelve months of the year are dispersed in all the right quarters pertaining to the sections of the year. The twelve fruits that are produced for each month of the year are to be seen carved amongst the seasonal foliage. Meanwhile, most of the gradually ageing Green Men present in the chapel are balanced by angels holding scrolls. These symbolise pages from books of ancient knowledge.

In Rosslyn Chapel, Biblical stories sit alongside kabalistic symbols, Old Testament, historical, moral and philosophical stories are depicted side by side, waiting to be translated and put into the context of their positioning. On the outside of the building, high in the North East finial is the carved beehive – which until very recently was always occupied by wild bees. It was said that in the summer honey made by the wild bees could be seen seeping down into the north-east corner of the roof, with the promise of sustenance and sweetness, as was prophesised by John the Baptist, and just as is mentioned in the story of St Matthew and the magic he wrought in Myrna.

The Chapel is dedicated to St Matthew, and for very good reason. The Hebrew Gospel of St Matthew was close to the heart of the Ebionites because it had eulogised John the Baptist and demonstrated that he had preceded Jesus as head of the Jerusalem sect. Finally Matthew was important because his feast day was on 21 September. 21 September in the original Julian calendar was also the all-important Autumn Equinox, as it is once again today.

The chapel was built to the most exacting standards and designed so that twice a year, at the time of the Spring and Autumn Equinox, light from the sun would flood directly into it through a specially made light box, acting as a sign that the Holy Shekinah was resident in the building, seasonally fulfilling through nature, the ancient, sacred covenant between God and Mankind. The light box may also have been used in a more secret sense to trap the light of the planet Venus at specific times, an adjunct to pre-Masonic ceremonies taking place there.

The choice of the pivotal period in September that is so important to Rosslyn Chapel was crucial. Not least, this represented this Jewish New Year and was also the time of year at which both the first and second Temples in Jerusalem had been dedicated. It also lay at the heart of the old Mystery religions such as that of Demeter and it occurred when the sun occupied the zodiac sign of Virgo, which was itself equated with the Shekinah.

Written into the carvings of Rosslyn Chapel were stories from the Old Testament, especially those related to the Jerusalem Temple. But there were New Testament stories too because the Ebionites did not question the existence of Jesus or his disciples; they merely disagreed about his status and with what the Roman Christians had done to the original story of the Jerusalem Church.

Carvings in the chapel relate to philosophical imperatives and in particular to the teachings of Aristotle. The physical paradise obvious in Rosslyn's carvings did not simply tell the story of St Matthew in Myrna or indeed that of the Garden of Eden. They also related to *Alexander's Journey to Paradise*, a book of natural philosophy. Other carvings at Rosslyn Chapel point to the *Secretum Secretorum*, a book specifically written to give advice to princes about how to live their lives and to govern their subjects with fairness, chivalry and honesty.

What rites and secret services once took place in the chapel at night, when the shutters were safely barred, or down in the Crypt that may well have been viewed as the 'womb' of the building, may remain forever a mystery to all of us. It is known that the Crypt did have its own altar and it was certainly used by the Sinclair family.

Looking around a world that is still awash with the blood of wars fought in the name of religion it seems a shame that we are still ignoring the message of Rosslyn Chapel, over half a millennium after its completion. It would afford a great sense of achievement to both of us if this book helped to carry Rosslyn's very special lesson to a world that has a genuine need for its spiritual knowledge. We would also be fulfilling our part of the mission that Earl William Sinclair and Sir Gilbert Haye set themselves 550 years ago – almost to the day that this book was completed.

Appendix 1

Baphomet

Whilst we were writing this book John had a wonderful insight regarding the word 'Baphomet'. It is so ingenious that we thought we would bring it to the attention of interested readers.

As mentioned in this book, when the Templars were outlawed and put on trial after 1307 one of the charges brought against them was that they worshiped a mysterious bearded, male head, known as Baphomet. When put through the linguistic wringer that is the ancient Jewish 'Atbash Cipher', Baphomet comes out as 'Sophia', said to mean wisdom. Sophia is also an alternative name for the Holy Spirit and so therefore synonymous with the 'Shekinah'. However, in terms of our own research and discoveries the word Baphomet itself seems to be an intriguing composite word that betrays the Templar's Kabalistic beliefs. For the sake of the exercise we add another 'm' to the word so that it becomes 'Baphommet'.

If we split the word into three we get Bap –hom – met. The first division is taken from 'Baptist', whilst the second is the Latin word 'Hom', meaning man. The third component is an abbreviation of the word 'Metatron', which is of course the male companion of the female Shekinah. Thus the word Baphomet is meant to represent (John the) Baptist, Man and

Metatron. In other words John the Baptist was a man who had bestowed upon him the knowledge and power of the Metatron (which of course is synonymous with the Shekinah) and was also the link between man and God in Heaven. John in turn brought down the Metatron to Jesus when he was baptised in the River Jordan. We can therefore see that the 'Holy Spirit' mentioned in the New Testament of the Bible is the same as Metatron/Shekinah.

Appendix 2

Dolly and the Double Helix

In the year 1996 an event took place at the famed Roslin Institute, just a stone's throw from Rosslyn Chapel, that stunned the world and surprised both of us for very different reasons. It was from the Institute that word came regarding the first successful cloning of a higher mammal. The creature in question was a sheep that became famous across the world as 'Dolly'. Dolly had been born as a result of human manipulation. She had not been conceived in the normal way but represented an absolutely faithful copy of another sheep, born to a surrogate mother. This marked a tremendous advance in human knowledge and the manipulation of genetics.

Dolly's birth at the Roslin Institute, as coincidental as it may have been, seemed particularly relevant to Rosslyn Chapel for a couple of reasons. Firstly it was the intensive rearing of sheep by the Cistercian monks and the farmers of the Knights Templar that led to Britain taking the lead in sheep breeding and woollen production. By the 15th century this had contributed in no small part to the fortune of the Sinclair family, a large proportion of which was expended on the building of Rosslyn Chapel.

It had also occurred to us very early in our research how much the

Princes Pillar, with its ornate spiralling vines, reminded us of the double helix of DNA upon which the whole blueprint of life is based. There seems to be no more fitting epitaph to the achievement of the scientists at the Roslin Institute than the Princes Pillar. This deeply kabalistic image had existed in the Chapel for over five centuries before this monumental breakthrough was achieved less than a mile away.

Index

The Fall

The evidence for a Golden Age, 6,000 years of insanity, and the dawning of a new era

STEVE TAYLOR

The Fall is one of the most notable works of the first years of our century, and I am convinced it will be one of the most important books of the whole century.– **Elias Capriles, International Journal of Transpersonal Studies**

Important and fascinating, highly readable and enlightening.
– **Eckhart Tolle**

9781905047208/1905047207 • 352pp £12.99 $24.95

The Light of Civilisation

How the vision of God has inspired all the great civilizations

NICHOLAS HAGGER

In the most monumental study of the history of civilizations for several generations, Nicholas Hagger describes the grand sweep of history in the style of Gibbon, Toynbee and Spengler.

An extraordinary book. – **David Gascoyne**

9781905047635/1905047630 • 656pp • 230×153mm £24.99 $49.95

Mayflower: The Voyage that Changed the World

ANTHEA AND JULIA BALLAM

This new account of the famous voyage of the Mayflower and the establishment of the Pilgrims in America is the clearest the most vivid I have ever read. This is a timeless, inspirational story that will be enjoyed by people of all ages: exciting, informative and beautifully retold.
– **Nigel Hamilton, biographer**

9781903816387/1903816386 • 160pp • 216×140mm £11.99 $17.95 cl.

Nostradamus
The Illustrated Prophecies
PETER LEMESURIER
2nd printing

A revelation. I am amazed by the translations' objectivity and Lemesurier's refusal to interpret the prophecies beyond what the text itself suggests. The handsomely produced book is a supremely important volume to stock in your store. – **New Age Retailer**

9781903816486/1903816483 • 512pp • 230×153mm • b/w and colour illustrations

£19.99 $29.95 cl.

Renewed by the Word
The Bible and Christian revival since the Reformation
JEREMY MORRIS

Renewed by the Word captures the restless, endlessly self-regenerating character of Christianity, rooted as it is in a particular body of texts

9781842981474/1842981471 • 160pp • 230×153mm £14.99 cl.

The Secret History of the West
The influence of secret organisations from the Renaissance to the 20th century
NICHOLAS HAGGER

If you think that the history of Western civilization is all about progressive leaps and bounds, with Utopian visions often ending in wars, then think again. Nicholas Hagger has produced an enticing narrative analysing the roots and histories of large and small revolutions since the Renaissance. – **Nexus**

9781905047048/1905047045 • 592pp • 230×153mm £16.99 $29.95

Sheep
*The remarkable story of the humble animal
that built the modern world*
ALAN BUTLER

The story of the sheep 'is' the story of humanity, a surprisingly exciting and gripping tale that deserves to be told. Spanning a vast period of time, it includes some of the most famous names that have been left to us by history, and many that deserve to better recognised.

9781905047680/1905047681 • 224pp £9.95 $19.95 cl.

The Syndicate
The story of the coming world government
NICHOLAS HAGGER
2nd printing

Finally, a solid book about this pressing matter, and refreshingly without the usual hysteria or excessive speculation. Hagger has done his homework and is initially just concerned with supplying extensive data. Upon this he builds his case: contrary to popular belief, the desire for world domination has never died down. – **Amazon Review**

9781903816851/1903816858 • 456pp • 230×153mm £11.99 $17.95

The Unknown Nostradamus
The true story of his life and work
PETER LEMESURIER

Readers seeking a balanced look at the controversial astrologer will do well to start here. – **Publisher's Weekly**

A "must-read" for anyone seeking to learn more about this remarkable figure... **Midwest Book Review**

9781903816325/1903816327 • 288pp • 230×153mm £17.99 $27.95 cl.
9781903816479/1903816475 £14.99 pb.

Warriors of the Lord
The military orders of Christendom

MICHAEL WALSH

Wonderfully accessible and well written. – **Publisher's Weekly**

Offers great breadth of knowledge in an enormously accessible and straightforward fashion ...an agreeable and satisfying introduction.
– **Library Journal**

9781842981078/1842981072 • 260pp • 280×210mm • full colour £19.99 cl.

The 7 Aha!s of Highly Enlightened Souls
How to free yourself from ALL forms of stress

MIKE GEORGE

7th printing

A very profound, self empowering book. Each page bursting with wisdom and insight. One you will need to read and reread over and over again! ...
Paradigm Shift

I totally love this book, a wonderful nugget of inspiration. – **PlanetStarz**

9781903816318/1903816319 • 128pp • 190×135mm £5.99 $11.95

God Calling
A devotional diary

A. J. RUSSELL

46th printing

"When supply seems to have failed, you must know that it has not done so. But you must look around to see what you can give away. Give away something." One of the best-selling devotional books of all time, with over 6 million copies sold.

9781905047420/1905047428 • 280pp • 135×95mm • US rights sold £7.99 cl.

The Goddess, the Grail and the Lodge
The Da Vinci Code and the real origins of religion
ALAN BUTLER
5th printing

This book rings through with the integrity of sharing time-honoured revelations. As a historical detective, following a golden thread from the great Megalithic cultures, Alan Butler vividly presents a compelling picture of the fight for life of a great secret and one that we simply can't afford to ignore. – **From the foreword by Lynn Picknett & Clive Prince**

9781903816691/1903816696 • 360pp • 230×152mm £12.99 $19.95

The Heart of Tantric Sex
A unique guide to love and sexual fulfilment
DIANA RICHARDSON
5th printing

The art of keeping love fresh and new long after the honeymoon is over. Tantra for modern Western lovers adapted in a practical, refreshing and sympathetic way. One of the most revolutionary books on sexuality ever written. ... **Ruth Ostrow, News Ltd**

9781903816370/1903816378 • 260pp • b/w+colour illustrations £19.95 $29.95

I Am With You
The best-selling modern inspirational classic
JOHN WOOLLEY
14th printing hardback

Will bring peace and consolation to all who read it. – **Cardinal Cormac Murphy-O'Connor**
9780853053415/0853053413 • 280pp • 150×100mm £9.99 cl.

4th printing paperback
9781903816998/1903816998 • 280pp • 150x100mm £6.99 $12.95

O

is a symbol of the world,
of oneness and unity. O Books
explores the many paths of whole-
ness and spiritual understanding which
different traditions have developed down
the ages. It aims to bring this knowledge in
accessible form, to a general readership, providing practical spirituality to today's seekers.

For the full list of over 200 titles covering:

ACADEMIC/THEOLOGY • ANGELS • ASTROLOGY/
NUMEROLOGY • BIOGRAPHY/AUTOBIOGRAPHY
• BUDDHISM/ENLIGHTENMENT • BUSINESS/LEADERSHIP/
WISDOM • CELTIC/DRUID/PAGAN • CHANNELLING
• CHRISTIANITY; EARLY • CHRISTIANITY; TRADITIONAL
• CHRISTIANITY; PROGRESSIVE • CHRISTIANITY;
DEVOTIONAL • CHILDREN'S SPIRITUALITY • CHILDREN'S
BIBLE STORIES • CHILDREN'S BOARD/NOVELTY • CREATIVE
SPIRITUALITY • CURRENT AFFAIRS/RELIGIOUS • ECONOMY/
POLITICS/SUSTAINABILITY • ENVIRONMENT/EARTH
• FICTION • GODDESS/FEMININE • HEALTH/FITNESS
• HEALING/REIKI • HINDUISM/ADVAITA/VEDANTA
• HISTORY/ARCHAEOLOGY • HOLISTIC SPIRITUALITY
• INTERFAITH/ECUMENICAL • ISLAM/SUFISM
• JUDAISM/CHRISTIANITY • MEDITATION/PRAYER
• MYSTERY/PARANORMAL • MYSTICISM • MYTHS
• POETRY • RELATIONSHIPS/LOVE • RELIGION/
PHILOSOPHY • SCHOOL TITLES • SCIENCE/
RELIGION • SELF-HELP/PSYCHOLOGY
• SPIRITUAL SEARCH • WORLD
RELIGIONS/SCRIPTURES • YOGA

Please visit our website,
www.O-books.net